"Here is what will happen as you read this book. You will learn more about how to love those who have lost someone, you will be loosened from your own calcifying grief, you will actually enjoy more of the love of God, you will notice hope growing, and you will cry—mostly all at the same time."

    **Ed Welch, PhD,** CCEF Faculty; psychologist; best-selling author

"This is a painful, but hopeful book to read. For those of us privileged to have known Al and Libbie as a couple, this book is a poignant reminder of a lost friend. But it is more than that. It is also a powerful plea for the reader to take seriously the truth of the gospel and a trenchant reminder of how Jesus Christ stands with his people in even the darkest of times and will bring them ultimately through death to their eternal home."

    **Carl Trueman,** Author; pastor; Paul Woolley Professor of Church
    History, Westminster Theological Seminary

"The great privilege of this book is getting an inside look, a sneak peak at a real working faith. The juxtaposition of Al and Libbie's faith and the realities they are facing gives the book an unusual, vibrant feeling. This book is soul food at its finest."

    **Paul Miller,** Director of seeJesus, author of *A Loving Life*

"I will never forget Al Groves's huge memorial service. The congregation was singing a praise song from the book of Job: '[God] gives and takes away; blessed be the name of the Lord.' Libbie's hand was stretched toward heaven, palm upward in worship, yielding Al to God. In this book, she yields him again. These pages are a godly woman's poignant offering to Jesus of her dearest earthly friend."

    **Steve Estes,** Pastor; author of *A Better December* and *When God Weeps*

"Here is a down-to-earth account of death through cancer, but written as a journey with God. It is a heart-wrenching, honest, and moving account of the joys and regrets of caring for a husband dying of cancer. Written in such an engaging style, the author enables the reader both to resonate with her pain and to marvel at the grace and mercy of God that captivated her and her husband. I read. I wept. I gave thanks to God."

    **The Most Rev. Dr. Glenn N. Davies,** Archbishop of Sydney, Australia

"'My grace is sufficient for you, for my power is made perfect in weakness.' This promise of Christ is not only for the apostle Paul, as this volume so convincingly and winsomely evidences. Though written in a highly personal vein, it does not so much draw attention to the author as it does to Christ's sustaining and sanctifying sufficiency. Here is hope and encouragement for Christians undergoing similar circumstances. *Grief Undone* indeed."

    **Richard B. Gaffin, Jr.,** Professor of Biblical and Systematic Theology,
    Emeritus, Westminster Theological Seminary

"Deepest joy and profoundest hope is often best seen through glistened eyes. This collection of brief but exceedingly poignant reflections on the death of one of the Lord's saints will have many readers thanking God with hearts weeping but overflowing because the subject is not ultimately Al's death or his family's journey through grief; it's about how the presence of Jesus bathes even the land of darkest sorrow in light."

**Dan McCartney,** Professor of New Testament Interpretation, Redeemer Theological Seminary

"In *Grief Undone*, the reader is given the most honest and vivid picture of the walk through the valley of the shadow of death that I have ever read. There is the depth of both the valley and the darkness. But in these brief and engaging chapters there is also the constant presence of the Shepherd whose triumph over death gives the reader true comfort to believe that 'I need not fear for thou art with me.'"

**Dr. Tim Witmer,** Professor of Practical Theology, Westminster Theological Seminary; pastor

"This book offers a touching testament to the power of love over death, one that does more than merely chronicle the journey of J. Alan Groves's battle with cancer, but that beautifully articulates the broad range of feelings, moods, sentiments, and longings his family faced throughout its long, painful ordeal. *Grief Undone* tells a tale of one family's journey with cancer and how it sensed God's quiet, compassionate presence at every turn."

**Rev. Dennis J. Billy, CSsR,** John Cardinal Krol Chair of Moral Theology at St. Charles Borromeo Seminary

"In this book Libbie expresses concern that she's not very open about what goes on inside or that she loves people well. Don't believe her. In her straightforward and down-to-earth way, she brings dying to life. She reveals the raw and the real within her own heart. She invites us into intimate moments with Al and with Jesus. We come away wanting to be a part of this faithful, loving family, and realize that in Jesus, we are."

**Jayne V. Clark, MAR,** Chief of Staff, CCEFoundation

"Al Groves was a mentor and friend to many people, and now his wife Libbie draws us into their private life with a mixture of intimacy, honesty, and practical theology. The result is simply inspiring. This whole book is 'vulnerably and excruciatingly beautiful,' to borrow one of her own phrases, so get ready to weep, laugh, think, and reflect along with her."

**Charles Clayton,** Director, Oxford Leaders Ltd; Chief Executive, Primary Care Trauma Foundation; Former Executive Director of World Vision International

"Libbie Groves invites us into her personal valley of death to help us see, hear, and feel *how* God comforts and strengthens his precious children. Instead of advising us how to avoid painful feelings, Libbie shows us how God walked her through the full range of human emotions that accompany the loss of a loved one in Christ. Our strong Savior disarms death, helps us face grief head-on with a sweet and certain hope of resurrection, and generously gives us himself in our deepest sorrow."

**Barbara R. Duguid,** Author of *Extravagant Grace*, Biblical Counselor, Speaker

"Having followed and loved the blog Al and Libbie published during Al's illness, I wondered how any narrative could be as riveting. But in this book Libbie masterfully weaves the blog's inspiring messages into a story of love, courage, and humor. It is a model of how to walk the path of suffering while staying connected to God as the source of strength."

**Amy Givler, MD,** author of *Hope in the Face of Cancer: A Survival Guide for the Journey You Did Not Choose*

"If you want to see the gospel in action, then retrace the steps of an ordinary family's bittersweet journey into the valley of the shadow of death. Bitter and tear-filled, for obvious reasons. Yet sweet and faith-filled, as they walk through the darkness, with eyes focused on the hope of resurrection and open to see the surprising ways God comforts them when facing the final enemy. Painful but profoundly encouraging!"

**Douglas Green, PhD,** Professor of Old Testament, Westminster Theological Seminary

"We struggle to give words to our experience of grief. In this book, Libbie has done a great service to all pilgrims who have laid another in the grave to await the resurrection from the dead. This is certainly a book to read slowly, prayerfully, and in conversation with others. It is deeply human and deeply heavenward at the same time. Read it and taste comingled grief and renewal. Just as the Psalms tell it and Al would have wanted it."

**Michael Kelly,** Professor of Old Testament, Westminster Theological Seminary.

"Anyone facing this path of loss and uncertainty could benefit from the generous openness of a wise and loving friend whose confidence in the Lord's faithfulness and constant presence has been forged in similar circumstances. Here is such a friend."

**Dr. Ruth Marshall,** Biblical Counselling UK

"In this memoir by Libbie Groves about her husband's death and her life beyond, she provides the reader many simple reminders of God's presence in dark times. However, the meditations from Al may have been my greatest delight. His observations about Psalm 22 and 23 alone are worth the price of the book. But read on, and see how God continues to meet Libbie in grief, joy, and most of all, the hope of heaven."

**Philip G. Monroe, PsyD,** Professor of Psychology & Counseling, Biblical Seminary

"In *Grief Undone*, Libby recounts her husband Al's battle with cancer and her subsequent journey as a widow and single mother. The book is an honest, encouraging read that doesn't minimize the heartache and agonizing pain of losing a loved one even as it testifies to the sustaining goodness of God and the hope of glory that lies ahead for Christians."

**Erika Moore,** Professor of Old Testament Studies and Hebrew, Trinity School for Ministry

"*Grief Undone* is heart-breaking—bringing me to tears as I walked through the 89 accounts of God's faithfulness to my great professor-mentor-friend, his wife Libbie, and their family; heart-warming—exhilarating as I saw how God's people celebrate his goodness; and heart-probing—daring me to face grief head-on in a whole new way. *Grief Undone* is extraordinary!"

**Michael Phua, Rev., PhD,** Associate Professor, Singapore Bible College

"This book not only allows us to journey with Libbie, Al, and their kids through the valley of the shadow of death, it pointedly drives us to the hope of resurrection we have in Jesus Christ. It is this hope that our dear friend Al Groves cherished even in the face of death."

**Dr. Hulisani Ramantswana,** Senior Lecturer, University of South Africa, Department of Biblical and Ancient Studies

"*Grief Undone* is an invitation to and an offer of a model by which we too can learn from the Lord enough to trust his loving heart and be able to stare any perturbing circumstance in the face courageously and see beyond it to the triumph of Calvary. I heartily recommend this book to anyone who lives in this fallen world with all its disappointments and tears."

**Rev. Cephas T. A. Tushima, PhD,** Associate Professor of Biblical Studies, Vice President for Academic Affairs, Jos ECWA Theological Seminary

# Grief Undone

## A JOURNEY WITH GOD AND CANCER

*Elizabeth W. D. Groves*

New
Growth
Press
WWW.NEWGROWTHPRESS.COM

New Growth Press, Greensboro, NC 27404
www.newgrowthpress.com

Cover Design: Faceout Books, faceoutstudio.com
Typesetting: Lisa Parnell, lparnell.com

ISBN: 978-1-939946-52-2 (Print)
ISBN: 978-1-939946-73-7 (eBook)

Library of Congress Cataloging-in-Publication Data
Groves, Elizabeth.
  Grief undone : a journey with God and cancer / Elizabeth W. D. Groves.
    pages cm
  ISBN 978-1-939946-52-2 (print) — ISBN 978-1-939946-73-7 (ebook)
1. Groves, Elizabeth. 2. Groves, Al, -2007—Health. 3. Cancer—Patients—United States—Biography. 4. Cancer—Patients—Religious life—United States. 5. Cancer—Patients—United States—Family relationships. I. Title.
  RC265.6.G76A3 2015
  362.19699'40092—dc23
  [B]
                                                        2014045419
Printed in the United States of America

22 21 20 19 18 17 16 15     1 2 3 4 5

*For Al,*

my husband and friend,

who lived justly, loved mercy, and walked humbly with his God.

(Micah 6:8)

# CONTENTS

# FOREWORD

It is a privilege to introduce *Grief Undone*. The story it tells is a poignant one: how the Groves family walked together through what the psalmist describes as "the valley of deepest darkness"—what most English translations call "the valley of the shadow of death." In this case, the shadow cast on each of the family's lives was the prolonged sickness and eventual death of Al Groves, their husband and father.

For Al, death has already been undone and become the gateway to life with Christ. For his family, the longer undoing—of grief—continued and continues. In these pages we are allowed into their shared pain and struggles, and all the discouragements of mortal illness—but yet in the midst of it all, we can sense moments when the atmosphere of heaven prematurely came to earth and visited and surrounded their lives.

If you are a reader who knew Al, or know any of his family, there will be moments when you will choke back your emotions—or, perhaps better, unashamedly allow them to flow in quiet tears in which the ache of loss and the joy of God's grace mingle together. If you belong to the much larger number who are introduced here to them for the first time, these pages will, I suspect, move you in an unusual way.

Al's dying and death form the plot-line of this narrative. He died well. But death is always "the last enemy." Its shadow falls inward and outward, forward and backward on those who love most and therefore lose most. We can never say to someone else in their grief: "I know what you are going through." All we know is what we went through, or are going through still. But there are needs we all share—the need to know that when we are in the dark valley the Lord really will be with us and walk us through it, however long it lasts.

Here *Grief Undone* confirms our fears, for the valley is dark and the pathway sore and difficult. But it also confirms Christ's promises: he will be with us; he will not turn us away when we come to him; he understands and will walk on with us, even when we cannot sense or see his presence.

At root *Grief Undone* is a love story—not only between a man and a woman, but within an entire family. And underneath it, surrounding it, and continuing in the ongoing story, is the love of Christ for his children, and the fact that he never, ever leaves them.

This is the story that awaits you as you turn these pages. I suspect that when you come to the end, you will be grateful the Groves family have allowed you into their lives and shared their story. Perhaps more than that, you will want to pause to renew your faith in their Lord and Savior and to rest in his love for you. That, I am sure, is what they would most want.

Sinclair B. Ferguson

# ACKNOWLEDGMENTS

It is hard to know where to start to thank so many people for their help.

This book is drawn from material on a blog that Al and I kept (www.algroves.info), although the two are substantially different, not only in shape and length but in content. Therefore it is appropriate to start by thanking Karyn Traphagen, who had the idea for that blog in the first place and who set it up and managed it for us. And Kirk Lowery who has hosted it and kept its technology updated.

Ruth Marshall patiently read my manuscript and gave me great input.

Sue Lutz was a phenomenal editor, giving me helpful and valuable direction and feedback at every point. Barbara Miller Juliani believed in this project, and the whole team at New Growth Press walked with me through the process.

Both Michael Rogers and my son Alasdair did me the favor of giving helpful feedback for my specific questions.

*So* many people loved us and were part of the process of the Lord "undoing" our grief. Our families and others who live at a distance loved, encouraged, and blessed us from afar. The many dear people who read the blog and wrote strengthening, encouraging comments constantly built our faith and reminded us that we were not alone. Our church family—New Life Church in Glenside, Pennsylvania—and many friends and neighbors who live nearby blessed us over and over again with service of every kind during Al's illness and in the years afterward. All of these people were constant evidence to us of God's tender love for us.

Al's mom and dad, Jim and Jacquie Groves, loved Al, taught him well, and raised him to be a man whose life and death are worth writing about.

Alasdair, Lauren, Rebeckah, Eowyn, and Alden offered me precious fellowship, love, faith, and solidarity as we all walked the road to Al's death together, and they have shown tender care for me in the years since. This is their story as much as Al's or mine. I could never capture in words how much their support and companionship has meant, but I think they know.

My sons-in-law, Brian and Ben, and my soon-to-be daughter-in-law, Taylor, are part of the continuation of the story and are living proof, along with my grandchildren, that Al was right—the Lord would indeed give me a rich future and would bring joy and delight into my life.

And of course, most importantly, Al, who gave me a lifetime of love. It is only because of the deep, simple, unshakable faith that God gave Al every step of the way that there is a story to tell in this book. I am so very grateful to Al for showing me what it looks like to live and die well.

# INTRODUCTION

In early 2006 my husband Al was diagnosed with malignant melanoma. It had spread to his lungs, and we knew from the moment of diagnosis that there was no cure for it. Barring a miracle, it would kill him. This book chronicles our family's journey during his battle with cancer.

Al and I have four children. At the time of Al's diagnosis, our son Alasdair was twenty-three and had been married to his wife Lauren for a year and a half. They were living in New Hampshire. Our daughter Rebeckah was twenty-one and a senior in college, also in New Hampshire. Eowyn, our younger daughter, was fourteen and in the ninth grade. And Alden, our younger son, was twelve, in seventh grade. Al was fifty-three and serving as the Academic Dean at Westminster Theological Seminary in Philadelphia, having taught Old Testament there for a quarter of a century. I was forty-eight and working on a master's degree at Westminster.

A year and a half earlier, when Al had had a melanoma scare that turned out well, he had emailed friends and family throughout the process to keep them updated and to ask them to pray for us.

When melanoma reared its head a second time, Al again emailed folks to ask for prayer. But sending multiple batch emails was cumbersome; there were always addresses that bounced and other glitches, and we inevitably missed people. Then our good friend Karyn set up a blog for us (www.algroves.info)—a novel thing at the time that turned out to be an incredible blessing. This book is different from that blog in length, shape, and some of the content, but a substantial amount of the material is drawn from it.

Al loved and delighted in people and formed close relationships. And he had taught and impacted students from literally around the globe. So when the blog went up and the news spread that Al was dying, people from every continent, as well as local friends, checked in and followed his journey. As a result, in addition to an incredibly supportive network of local friends, we were also blessed with a worldwide community who loved and encouraged us. If you go to the blog and read the comments, you'll see what I mean.

I'm sure you can imagine the blessing that both communities—local and cyber—were to us. What was surprising to us was that people said it was a blessing to them as well! Evidently they found it encouraging to be a part of someone's day-to-day journey through terminal cancer and to read about medical symptoms and scriptural reflections, sorrow and joy, pain and glory, humdrum life details, simple faith, stretching moments, hidden blessings, and most of all how *God was with us*.

As I look back from this distance, several years later, my single, overriding impression is just that: that God was with us in every possible way. He fed our souls from the Bible. His Holy Spirit spoke to our hearts and reminded us of his wonderful promises. And he loved us through people who helped and supported us. Apparently he blessed others too, as they joined us on the journey, whether in the flesh or via the blog.

I hope that as you read these pages, you too will see God intimately, tenderly present with his people and that you will come away refreshed, encouraged, and blessed by him.

I have intentionally kept most of the chapters short, knowing that some of you who read this may be in the midst of grief.

# LIFE BEFORE

# 1

# Bookends

June 17, 1978, was a beautiful, clear, sunny day with wispy clouds and a gentle breeze. Al and I stood in Rollins Chapel in Hanover, New Hampshire, surrounded by family and friends, and pledged our love and faithfulness to each other for "as long as we both shall live." At the reception, The Old Time Fiddlers rosined up their bows, and the square dancing began.

"You still have frosting in your mustache."

"Do I?"

"Yup."

"I love you."

"I love you too. Always."

♣

Twenty-eight and a half years later, February 9, 2007, was bitterly, wickedly cold—uncharacteristically so for Pennsylvania—with an arctic wind that whipped across the snow and numbed our faces and toes. My groom, barely fifty-four, bald from radiation treatments and bearing the six-month-old remnants of a black eye from brain surgery, was just lowered into the frozen ground. Until today I hadn't ever stayed around a burial site long enough to hear the lid of the concrete grave liner drop shut with its loud and decisive thud, but I heard it this time. I winced and wished that our children and Al's parents hadn't heard that sound.

He really is gone.

"Good-bye, my friend. I love you. I'll see you soon."

The new chapter—the solo widow and fatherless children chapter—begins.

# 2

# The Story Before the Story

Of course there was a story before the story of Al's melanoma. Things that each of us had previously experienced, thought, discovered, or believed contributed to who we were when we learned that Al had terminal cancer.

I don't think I spent too much time during my childhood thinking about death. I recall crying and being distressed at one point about the thought that my parents could die. When I was about ten, my grandmother, who was my favorite person in the whole world at the time, passed away, and I remember being emotionally blindsided by her funeral. But apart from those experiences and perhaps occasionally wondering about what happened to people after they died, death was not frequently on my mind.

As a young teenager I discovered that God was real. I was enthralled with so many things about him and astonished at what he had done for me in Jesus's death and resurrection: he gave me love, forgiveness, and acceptance, made me part of a worldwide family, enlisted me in a cause that was worth living and dying for . . . the list could go on and on. But even at the age of thirteen, one of the most precious things to me was that Jesus had set me free from death. I don't mean that I wouldn't physically die, but that dying would just be a door into life with him that would be more glorious than I could get my head around. Being able to *know* that with certainty took away any fear of death I had; in fact I even started looking forward to it! Not to the physical process of dying, of course, but to living the glorious life on the other side of it. The Baptist church I attended must have focused a lot on the glories of heaven ahead. I didn't know at the time that this was unusual, but I think it instilled in me from a young age an anticipation and excitement about being in heaven—something I have been thankful for in recent years. At the time a friend and I sometimes talked about how excited we were to go to heaven, and I think that worried our parents. But honestly, the hope of heaven made a happy difference in life here.

Al and I shared that outlook. Freedom from fearing death's power was a precious thing to both of us long before we faced his death sentence. In 1979, his grandfather died unexpectedly the day before we were leaving on a trip to visit him. Al found he had three competing emotions: *I'm so sad we're not going to see him. I'm suddenly absolutely certain that Grandpa is in heaven and that I'll see him again. And I kind of envy him in a way—that he's getting to see Jesus face-to-face.* I think Al was surprised by the envy. Perhaps it was the first time he became aware of longing to be in God's presence.

Over the years our picture of God steadily grew, and we realized more and more how majestic, glorious, powerful, good, holy, loving, and tender he was. We understood increasingly that he ruled over all things, and that sometimes he allowed—even brought—suffering into the lives of his children for a high and holy purpose. And we saw firsthand in the lives of others how he was always intimately present with them in that suffering. The longer we each walked through life with Jesus as our companion, friend, and king, and the better we got to know him, the more that quiet longing to see him face-to-face increased. We thoroughly enjoyed the many blessings of this life and were in no hurry to leave it, especially once we had children, but in the background there was always also the quiet sense that the best life by far lay on the other side of the grave.

In October of 1993, a good friend of ours died suddenly from a heart attack. He had known and walked with Jesus for many years, so we knew exactly where Ray woke up after he died. As I thought about Ray, I found that I imagined heaven in a lot more detail. I pictured Ray alive, healthy, dancing in worship, filled with irrepressible joy in the presence of the King. I also found that heaven seemed vividly real—almost more so than the world that my physical eyes saw daily.

That fresh nearness of heaven inevitably faded, pressed out by the bustle and demands of life. But apparently the Lord locked it away in my memory, ready to be revived when needed. I never guessed that I would need it because my husband was going to die.

# 3

# Out of Danger

Melanoma is a type of skin cancer. When it is found in the top layers of the skin, it can be easily removed and poses no further threat. No chemo or radiation is necessary because the cancer is entirely gone. However, if melanoma penetrates the skin layers to enter the body, it is often deadly. It tends to travel to the lymph system, and from there it spreads to organs—most often the lungs, liver, and brain.

In 2003 Al had a spot removed from his shoulder and biopsied. It showed no malignancy. In 2004 the spot grew back. It was removed and biopsied again, and at that point the pathology was unclear. Were the abnormalities potentially melanoma or just scar tissue, and in either case, how deep did they go? In order to be certain and to remove any possibility of lingering cells, a more extensive surgery was performed, removing a patch of skin several inches long and almost an inch wide. The "sentinel lymph nodes" closest to the excision site were also removed and tested to see if any melanoma, if that's what it was, had spread to the lymph system.

Al later told me that he would occasionally look at his hands during that time and marvel at their intricate design. He wondered what it would be like to die and not need those hands anymore, for them to be lifeless.

But the report from the surgery was that everything was clear—all the skin margins and lymph nodes. *We were so relieved!* One night a few weeks later I was sitting at Al's desk after he had gone to bed, writing a poem for him for Christmas, which is our tradition. I could hear him breathing regularly in the loft above me, and as I looked at his glasses folded next to the computer, I thought about what it would have been like if the report had been bad. What if Al had died and his eyes didn't need those glasses anymore? The thought simultaneously broke my heart and left me overwhelmingly grateful that it was not true.

We were all thankful to be out of those woods. Al had a routine chest X-ray in January 2005, which showed that his lungs were clear, as expected. He would continue to be monitored—several visual skin checks per year and one annual chest X-ray to confirm that the lungs were clear—but that was just a precaution. We were not really worried.

# WINTER '06

# 4

# Holding onto Hope

On a late Monday afternoon in January 2006, I had just come home from grocery shopping, giving blood, and picking up Rebeckah's bridesmaid dress. I ordered pizza because there simply hadn't been time in the day to make supper, and also because a young woman had just moved in with us that day, and we wanted to celebrate her arrival.

As Al helped me unload groceries, he tried to sound casual when he said with the tiniest odd note in his voice, "The hospital called. They said there was a spot on my chest X-ray."

I looked up sharply and caught my breath. Something inside me suddenly tightened up and felt cold. We continued to unload groceries as he filled me in on a string of medical appointments that had already been lined up, but I couldn't pull my mind back from racing down dark and scary paths. I remembered hearing years earlier about some-one who discovered he had melanoma and died of it six weeks later. Was that what we were facing? Would Al be gone in six weeks? I could hardly get my mind around the thought. There was an empty feeling in my gut, and my breathing was fast and shallow. I remember trying to keep my voice calm and normal as we talked, partly because that's how I operate in crises, and probably also because I didn't want to betray my alarm over how serious this might be. I didn't want to convey the fear *If it's melanoma, you might die!* Maybe he was thinking the same thing and being calm for my sake.

The week was filled with multiple doctors' appointments as well as the usual daily routines. I kept thinking about what life would be like without Al if he died, how terribly much I would miss him, and all the ways I wanted to love him better. I cried so often that my head ached and my eyes felt like sandpits. Al and I talked about logistics and schedules, and a bit about implications, but I think we each wanted to spare the other thinking too much about the full ramifications of how dire the situation might be.

On Wednesday we told our kids the news. We had always tried to be as honest and straightforward with our kids as we could, and I think they appreciated that. From the time they were old enough to understand death, we had been open about the fact that life is uncertain and we could not promise things like "I'll always be here" or "I'm not going to die." Those things sound comforting, but they lie outside our control, and hence can end up proving untrue. Sometimes parents *do* die. Instead, we had encouraged them to trust God, who loves them, who is in control over all things, and who will *always* be there, no matter what. That is something we know will hold true. Both we and they needed to find our comfort and assurance there, not in promises we couldn't keep. So we told them the situation.

It's hard to tell your kids that their father has something that might turn out to be terminal cancer. I wished we didn't have to burden them with news like that! I watched them closely, and my heart ached for them as they absorbed the situation—as much as you can absorb in the first hour of processing such news, especially at twelve and fourteen. They were brave. They asked questions. Soberly, maybe taking their lead from us, they connected to the hope of heaven and the reality of life beyond the grave. And then we prayed together for mercy, for healing, for peace.

That night, January 19th, Al wrote the following in an email to friends:

> Once again my family and I are in a place where we need your prayers. [He then explained about the X-ray results and ended by saying] At the moment, I can say the Lord has given us great peace in the matter, though it has challenged us at moments more than the original melanoma did. We have been much comforted by reminders that he is our salvation and refuge. Mostly we are resting in him. God can heal. He alone heals! And he alone gives grace to face any trial. We will receive with joy what he has to give us.

A CAT scan gave us more details about the mass in Al's lung and revealed that there were actually three of them—one in the left lung and two in the right. We wouldn't know for sure what the spots were until a biopsy was done, but I felt certain they were melanoma. What else could they be? My fears felt increasingly well-founded, and danger seemed inescapable.

# 5

# One at a Time, Please!

Exactly two weeks after the initial call about Al's chest X-ray came a day that was particularly difficult. Al and I took the train down to the Hospital of the University of Pennsylvania (HUP) to see a doctor who specialized in melanoma. We still did not have a biopsy, so the doctor could not say anything conclusive, but he outlined the possible diagnoses, all malignant.

Al asked, "How about benign possibilities?"

The doctor gazed at the ceiling in thought for a moment and then said, "I'm not coming up with any."

That was sobering for Al. On the train ride home, he commented that the doctor didn't seem very optimistic. I was surprised at Al's surprise. It was what I had expected. Apparently he had been able to entertain the idea that it might turn out to be nothing serious. Al was optimistic by nature.

At dinner we got a call saying that the president of a Korean seminary and two other people wanted to come by to say hello. We scrambled to find something to serve them with tea, and Eowyn, Alden, and the young woman who had just moved in retreated to the kitchen to do the dishes. The president was quite insistent in talking to Al about coming to teach in Korea in June. Al tried to say "Thank you, but I can't" graciously, without giving an explanation, since we didn't know exactly what his medical condition was. All I could think as I listened was, "Will Al still be *alive* in June? Will he even be alive in March?" The whole conversation felt surreal.

Just as our guests were leaving, the phone rang. Al was waving goodbye from the front steps as I answered it. It was the son of our dear friends in Amsterdam, Eep and Lies, telling us that Lies had just died. She had had a slow-growing cancer for years, and before Al's lung issues surfaced, I had hoped to visit her in February or March.

The day's sorrows had mounted, and we felt weighed down with sadness on top of sadness. We hugged each other and cried about Lies.

"I can't believe she's gone. I really hoped to see her next month. After so long, all of a sudden it went fast." Our unspoken thought was, *Is this what we are facing? What will that be like?*

"Should we try to go to the funeral?"

"Can we? What about all your medical tests? Don't those need to happen as soon as possible?"

"I'm sure delaying a week won't be the end of the world."

"What about the kids?"

"We'll see if we can find somebody to stay with them."

"But this seems like a terrible time to leave them."

"They'll be okay."

"Can we afford it? Last-minute flights are expensive."

"We'll see. Let's at least explore the possibilities."

(Pause) "Do you think we should tell Eep about your situation or wait until later, after he's had some time to grieve?"

(Longer pause) "I don't know." (We did end up waiting to tell him.)

Al wrote in an email that night:

I'll be honest. I feel quite emotionally drained at this point, given the news of Lies's death and all that is connected with my own situation. Still I would be remiss if I did not say that God has sustained and has been so good.

# 6

## The Only Certain Thing

It took five weeks to get a definitive confirmation of melanoma, partly because you can't fly after a needle biopsy because of changes in air pressure, so the biopsy had to be postponed until we returned from Lies's funeral. It was a time of uncertainty, and uncertainty is hard for us humans.

I remember at one point biking along behind Al in the rain, looking at his back and thinking, *I can't believe that Al might have terminal cancer. He looks and seems fine.*

He himself remarked, with a funny smile, that it was odd to think that "there might be something lurking in my body that doesn't have my best interests at heart."

It was strange to be in Amsterdam for Lies's funeral and to think that Al's might well follow. We had done a little research and learned that once melanoma has metastasized to major organs, life expectancy is about eleven months on average. The tumors in his lungs could have started growing any time between January 2005 and January 2006, so we didn't know how far into that eleven months we might already be.

On the one hand, I think we were impatient to know for sure what the situation was. And yet part of us didn't really want to know, assuming the news would be bad. Once we heard it, would we wish we could be back in the time of not knowing, when there was still hope for a good outcome? A friend who has a child with substantial health issues told me, "Enjoy this time when you don't know yet. This may be the happiest you're going to be for a long time." I don't think she meant it in a hopeless, pessimistic, Eeyore-ish way. I think it was more along the lines of Jesus's instruction not to worry about tomorrow, since each day has enough trouble of its own (Matthew 6:34).

I had to keep reminding myself of the truth we had always taught our kids: Our lives are in God's hands. If it is not the time for you to die, then you can spend three days floundering in shark-infested waters and you will survive. If it is the time appointed for you, then you can drown in a teaspoon of water. Our lives are not ruled by chance; we are in God's hands. We have comfort in knowing God as a loving Father who always chooses the best for us.

Daily and hourly we set our hope in the certainty of our Father's love in the midst of uncertainty about what would happen to Al. I don't know that that was a measured, intellectual decision on our part as much as it was just the natural cry of desperate children who know their Father is the only one who has answers and help.

# 7

# Life Will Never Be the Same

Five weeks and many tests and appointments after the initial phone call about the chest X-ray, we were finally on our way to see the melanoma specialist at Penn with whom we would work if the masses in Al's lungs did turn out to be melanoma. We got caught in construction traffic, so Al jumped out of the car and ran the last ten blocks or so. Results of the biopsy were not yet available when we left for the appointment, so we were still in the land of uncertainties, but we knew that some sort of clarity would come soon.

When we met with Dr. Schuchter, she was surprised that we still didn't have the result and got permission to call and check again. The report had just been finished, and so it happened that poor Dr. Schuchter, whom we had just met a few minutes earlier, was the one who had to give us the bad news. The masses were indeed melanoma.

Both of us wanted—and asked for—the full brunt and weight of the truth. We did not want Dr. Schuchter to hide or sugarcoat the situation and, to our great relief, she did not. She was professional, compassionate, straightforward, and clear. We were thankful for that.

When we asked her how long someone might expect to live once melanoma had metastasized to the major organs, she answered, "One of my patients in a similar situation lived for ten years."

Al sensed that that sounded like an unusual case and asked, "What would a more usual life expectancy be?"

"Most often one to two years."

I was very grateful for her honesty. And I started to quietly cry. I didn't want to. This poor woman was in an unenviable spot, and I really didn't want to make her feel any worse, but the tears just kept silently leaking out of my eyes. I couldn't stop them. I don't know what Al was thinking, but I thought, *If Al dies in two years, Eowyn and Alden will not even be out of high school. He won't see them graduate or go to college. He won't be here for their weddings. He won't even be here through their teens. Hopefully he'll be alive to see Rebeckah graduate from college in June, but he won't walk her down the aisle someday when she gets married. He won't see what our children grow up to be and do. If we have grand-children someday, he won't know them or even meet them.*

I had to stop thinking down those tracks and bring my attention back to what Dr. Schuchter was saying. She explained why surgery and other options were not practical in this case, but said that there was a clinical trial that Al would qualify for. It combined traditional chemotherapy with a newly developed targeted molecular therapy. As she explained how it worked, it gave us something specific and positive to think about, as well as a sense that there was something we could *do*.

At one point Dr. Schuchter left the room for just a second. We didn't say anything, but as I quietly cried, Al reached over and put his hand on top of mine and squeezed it.

Dr. Schuchter didn't hide the fact that there was no cure for Al— all things being equal, he would die from this melanoma. But the hope was that the clinical trial would put the brakes on the cancer for a while and thereby prolong the time he would live. "Progression-Free Survival" it is called, PFS. The goal was to make the cancer halt for as long as possible, even though at some future point it would eventually become active again and progress to its inevitable end.

# 8

# It's Always Okay to Cry

Al was able to register for the trial immediately. He took care of the initial blood work and other preliminaries that very day so that he could start the medication right away. While he was busy going from one room to another on those errands, I sat in the waiting room and tried not to cry. It was a large, busy practice in a large university hospital, so there were lots of people in and out of the multiple waiting rooms. And since this was a cancer office, many of them were probably dealing with similar diagnoses. I was sure it wasn't helpful to have a woman sitting there crying, so I really tried not to. But it was no use. I cry easily and always have, and in that moment, the silent tears just wouldn't stop.

On the way home we stopped and got cheesesteaks and then sat in the car and called our older children to tell them the news. "We got the biopsy results, and it's definitely melanoma . . . I'm in a clinical trial. . . Probably a year or two." I was okay until I heard Alasdair and Rebeckah break down in tears. One of the hardest things about this whole journey has been seeing our children in the pain of grief, and that was the first time I had experienced it. There would be many, many more such times in the next couple of years. Afterward Al and I both cried, and we talked about how hard it was to hear the grief in their voices, to hear our kids' hearts breaking. At dinner we broke the news to Eowyn and Alden.

There are, of course, many reasons that parents with cancer might not tell their kids about it. Maybe there is excellent hope for a cure and there will be minimal impact from treatments. Maybe the parents themselves are terrified of death and have no hope to offer their children. But since we knew that Al's cancer was terminal, and since we had a sure hope of heaven that made death sad but not scary, we had no doubts about the importance of being completely open and honest with our kids. So we talked about it and answered their questions. And we talked about and explained the clinical trial. Eowyn said, "Oh, targeted molecular therapy? We learned about that in biology." In fact she rattled off its initials, which I can no longer remember.

We also said, "Hey, new ground rule from now on: it is *always, always* okay to cry." I've been thankful for the freedom to cry as needed, and I think it has freed others, even those outside the family, to cry with us as well.

Afterward, Al and I talked.

"Oh man, that was hard."

"Yeah. It's going to be tough for them."

"It was neat that Eowyn already knew about the targeted therapy stuff."

"I know. That was thoughtful of the Lord, wasn't it? That Mr. Hartwell is a great teacher."

"This is going to be hard."

"I know. But the Lord will get us through it."

I don't know what it is like to find out that your dad is going to die when you are age twelve or fourteen or twenty-one or twenty-three, but it was a tough day.

Al told our friend Ed that night, "Nothing has changed." He meant in terms of God still being our Father who loved us and who always, *always* chose what was best for us—and who alone knew what "best" really meant. Al was right. Not a shred of that had changed, even as we knew that we were launched on a journey that would probably stretch us to our limits and that would look very different from anything we had ever envisioned.

# 9

# Facing Sadness, Facing God

The next weeks were challenging. Al had severe reactions to the molecular therapy, the worst of which were deep bruises and flaming blisters on his feet. At first, he could tough it out and push through the pain, but as the blisters and bruising progressed, he had to stop driving. Then he could barely hobble, and finally he couldn't walk at all and had to crawl to the bathroom.

Al always had a very high pain threshold, probably because he had been battling fibromyalgia for many years. It left him in constant pain and he never slept deeply, so he was chronically exhausted. He couldn't concentrate easily because of the brain fog, which was like a bad jet lag that never went away. Yet it never occurred to him to slow down for such things because he wanted to live as full a life as possible. He persevered like no one I've ever met. So when these side effects kicked in, he kept us informed about symptoms, but he didn't complain; he just kept soldiering on. He was thankful that at least the chemo side effects were minimal.

We sent out a query to see if anyone had a wheelchair we could borrow, and suddenly we had four! Al began to get around only in a wheelchair, and Alden became impressively good at doing wheelies in them.

Dr. Schuchter was phenomenal. She was visibly horrified by the blisters on his feet and declared his quality of life unacceptable. Over the next couple of months she carefully oversaw stopping and restarting the medication at different dosages to minimize the side effects.

Al was used to pushing through pain to do what he had to do, but with the onset of the cancer and the effects of the medication, he finally had to stop working at Westminster. That was hard for him. He loved his job, his colleagues, his students, his teaching. He would have loved to carry on there. Losing daily contact with the seminary community was painful for him, and he talked about how much he would miss the people there.

We started planning practical matters on the home front—for the immediate time and for a future time when Al would be gone. Thankfully, he had disability insurance and Westminster was generous in all the arrangements, so we were able to survive financially after he stopped working. We were enormously thankful for that. Our conversation included things like the following:

"Here is where to find our life insurance policies."

"What will I need to do to continue our health insurance through COBRA?"

"Erik can advise you on handling the insurance payments wisely and about what should happen to my pension."

"Do we need to do anything about the car title, house deed, or bank accounts, since they are all held jointly in both of our names?"

"Who do you think I should ask for advice about future car or home maintenance or replacing a computer?" (Al bought a new laptop before he died, I think partly to give me a few years before I would need to think about that.)

"Here's how my computer files are organized, and how you should sort/cull/delete them."

"I'll teach you how to do our taxes."

It was sobering and I did a lot of crying. It seemed impossible that he would really be gone.

I think Al was calm and matter-of-fact about it all because he wanted to be strong for me. And, as we planned, it reminded him of the resources God would provide: life insurance, yes, but more than that the people he knew would come alongside us. Plus, Al was a plan-ahead/action kind of guy, and this was something concrete and helpful he could do to prepare for our future without him. For my part, I knew it grieved Al to think of leaving us behind without his presence, support, help, and income. And I knew God would be faithful to us and take care of us and provide for us as he always had. So I talked about that to reassure Al that we would be okay. In fact, we kept reassuring each other of it.

In my own heart I tried to face each sadness squarely and then set it in the context of the bigger picture of God's love, of his promises, of the wonderful eternity we would enjoy with him. Holding the present sadness and the future hope in my heart at the same time was hard, but it did help.

# 10

## Overload

For me, there were times over the course of the year when the pressures simply became too much. Three particular weekends stand out.

The first was that week in early March when Al was increasingly unable to walk because of the blisters. It was also the week of the kids' school play, so I was back and forth between home and the junior high, filming dress rehearsals and the like. Our elderly neighbor, who had no family and few contacts in the area, ended up in the hospital and needed me to bring her various things from home. Eowyn's fifteenth birthday was that week, which involved a party with lots of friends and a special meal, as well as the usual family dinner and gifts. And we had overnight guests who came from out of town to see the kids' performance. Each of those things was a joy in its own right (except for my poor neighbor), but piled on top of each other, and on top of regular daily life, and on top of life-with-cancer, they became overwhelming. By the end of the week I was on complete overload and, being by nature an introvert, felt as if I wanted to crawl into a hole and not speak to another human for a long time.

Someone later asked why I attempted to do all those things under the circumstances, so I tried to reflect back on it. I think there were three reasons.

First, in the case of my neighbor, there was only one other person who knew her well and could have taken the things to her in the hospital. That woman lived some distance away, whereas I lived right across the street.

Second, I guess my approach to life had always been, "Do what needs to be done, whether that is convenient or not." It would have seemed selfish, or negligent, or irresponsible to me to pass that job off to someone else, and Catherine (the elderly neighbor) might have felt slighted had I done so. I don't think it ever occurred to me that I was in a situation in which it might have been legitimate to say, "Despite the distance, could you please drive over here and take Catherine's things to her?" At the time I probably didn't realize how overloaded I was.

And third, I knew how important many of these things were to Eowyn. I tended to go to great lengths for my kids' sakes anyway, and that was all the more true in the midst of Al's cancer. I tried to keep life as normal as possible. I knew it was hard enough for them that their dad was dying, and that right then he was also clearly in a lot of pain. I thought it would be even worse if I could no longer make special things happen for them. In retrospect, that might have been the wrong call. I'm sure they would have understood if we had had to curtail special events in light of Al's situation. Perhaps I didn't give them enough credit. Probably they would have taken such things in stride. But at the time the mother in me wanted to minimize their pain and maximize their enjoyment of life's good things.

A woman in our church had died a few years earlier, and during the course of her illness, friends had gathered in her home every week to pray for her. On our way to a doctor's appointment downtown, Al said, "What do you think about having people come over to our house to pray once a week the way they did for Linda?"

I'm sure it would have blessed Al if we had done that, and it probably would have blessed the pray-ers, and me too. But he happened to make the suggestion at the end of that overloaded week, and the thought of having even one person come to our house for one minute, much less lots of people on a weekly basis, was more than I could possibly think about. My response was, "No way! Absolutely not." I don't remember explaining to Al *why* I shot the idea down so definitively. Did he understand that it was because I had pushed myself too far over the edge? I don't know. I'm not even sure *I* fully realized that. I might have been beyond rational thought at that point.

I should have reconsidered the question once I got some sleep, had some time alone, and regained some perspective, but I never did. I regret that. It was perhaps understandable that I felt overwhelmed that particular week, and it was probably wise not to try to put the suggestion into action right away. But I'm sorry that we never revisited the idea, which prevented that blessing. Our usual way of approaching things was (1) Al would have an idea, (2) I would not be on board at first, (3) eventually I would come around, (4) we would do it, and (5) it would be great. Ordinarily Al would have brought an idea up again. In retrospect, I'm kind of surprised that he didn't. Maybe my no was uncharacteristically forceful; maybe he didn't realize that it was just due to my being temporarily jangled into dysfunction; maybe he didn't know I would have been open to reconsidering it later.

Looking back on the year Al was dying, there are things that I'm glad we did and things that I regret. This is one I'm sorry about.

# 11

# Peace in the Storm

God may be invisible to our physical eyes, but when we ask, the Holy Spirit does give us eyes of faith to see God as he is in heaven, seated on his throne, ruling the whole universe. When I pray, I picture myself kneeling before his throne. The amazing thing is that that's not just imagination; there is a sense in which that is exactly true.

There are two passages in the Bible that are linked in my mind—even if not in anyone else's—that comfort me when things are hard. The first, which some people find cold and harsh but I find encouraging, is Job 1:20–21: "Then Job arose and tore his robe and shaved his head and fell on the ground and worshiped. And he said, 'Naked I came from my mother's womb, and naked shall I return. The LORD gave, and the LORD has taken away; blessed be the name of the LORD.'" Job had just heard one crushing piece of bad news after another, culminating with the report that all ten of his children had been killed in a single disaster. Yet he fell at the Lord's feet and worshiped. That says something about Job. But I think it says even more about Job's God.

Job's God is also my God. He is so big, so mighty, and so powerful and full of majesty that he is worthy of worship no matter *what* he does. Even if he were malicious, his raw power alone would inspire awe. But he is also so giving, loving, and radically committed to me as his child—whom he sought out, rescued, and adopted that he gave up his own Son for me. And he is so kind, tender, compassionate, gracious, and faithful, that he, *the God of the universe*, walks with me through everything I face. He may set a hard path for my feet, as he did for Job, but he will walk every step of it with me and bring redemption out of it to display his great mercy.

*That* is a God I can trust. That is a God I can worship—even when from my perspective things seem hard or confusing or out of control. Kneeling at his feet and resting in the knowledge that he is the Lord of all—including my difficult circumstances—brings a quieting, shielding, empowering peace.

The second passage I think of as similar is Psalm 123:1–2, which says, "To you I lift up my eyes, O you who are enthroned in the heavens! Behold, as the eyes of servants look to the hand of their master, as the eyes of a maidservant to the hand of her mistress, so our eyes look to the LORD our God, till he has mercy upon us."

I remember someone telling me about a photo contest comprised of pictures of "peace." There were lovely sunsets, quiet woods, and serene lakes. But the winning photo was of a raging, crashing, wind-whipping, rain-lashing thunderstorm and a little squirrel curled up in its snug hole in a tree, warm and dry, sleeping undisturbed through the tempest.

That's something like the peace I find at God's feet in the midst of hard things. In fact, it's especially when things are hard that I need to be there, and there is no better place to be. When I spend time in God's throne room, amazed at the glorious and majestic, powerful and good God who sits on the throne of the universe and yet knows me intimately and loves me with a fatherly tenderness that I'll never fully grasp, it helps put things in much better perspective. Like the servants who look to the hand of their master, waiting until God has mercy upon them, I kneel quietly before him to take in his glory, marvel at his grace, soak up the bright light of his presence, dare to gaze into his eyes, and see there the smile, the love, and the welcome of my Father. When I do that, the clouds break, the weight lifts, and I remember what—or rather, Who—life is about, and that I am safely in his hands.

During college I was in a fellowship group where I learned some wonderful things about God. There was a keen sense of immediacy in worship. We pictured ourselves singing, or kneeling, or dancing before God's throne. I find that I often think in images and that they help me "put feet on" my walk with God. For instance, as followers of Jesus, we have the privilege of being servants of God. So sometimes I start the day kneeling by my bed, picturing myself as a servant in the ancient world, putting myself at my master's disposal, checking in to see what he would like me to do that day. It helps me remember to hold my plans loosely and let him redirect them if he chooses and to listen for his prompting as opportunities come up to love or bless someone.

Being in God's throne room is an image that helps me a lot. At the beginning of Al's cancer, in the midst of stress, worry, and anxiety about the future, I had a feeling that in the months ahead, occasional visits to the throne room would not suffice. Of course, that is true for all of us all the time anyway. I realized that my heart needed to take a sleeping bag and move in to God's throne room and stay.

# 12

# Flossing as an Act of Hope

With Al's cancer we discovered that in the face of a life-threatening illness you live in a tension between battle and acceptance.

How do we find the balance between holding onto life here and looking forward to life in heaven? Sometimes I hear about someone fighting valiantly to stay alive in the face of a deadly illness, and I admire him. I cheer for cancer survivors and for their will to live. Other times I hear about someone who knew she was going to die and faced that calmly and serenely, and I marvel at her faith and composure. Is one "right"? Is one better?

On the one hand, is it right to pray boldly for a miraculous healing? I would say yes. On the other hand, is it right to accept the cold, hard reality of a terminal diagnosis and walk toward death with faith and grace? I would say yes. Should we treasure life here on earth? Yes. But should we also look forward to heaven with anticipation? Yes. The two mind-sets may appear to be mutually exclusive, but I think that in Christ we can actually do both at the same time. We can fully treasure life and do all that reasonably lies within our power to preserve it, while at the same time resting in the knowledge that our lives are in God's hands and when he chooses to take us home, we can let go of this life and gladly embrace the better one ahead. That is how Al felt.

We knew from the beginning that Al's cancer was terminal so we were spared the emotional roller coaster that many cancer patients face of enduring a grueling treatment and hoping it will cure them only to see those hopes dashed if it proves ineffective. I think the rest of us would have foregone the clinical trial Al put himself through, with its painful side effects, since we knew it didn't hold any hope of curing him. He thought if it prolonged his life a bit it was worth it.

Thankfully, as we wrestle with trying to hold both sides of the tension in our hearts, we are not alone. We have the Lord's companionship, and we also have the church, the body of Christ. Holding each other up in prayer is part of the calling of the body of Christ. The Lord did not give me faith to believe that he would heal Al, rather that he was calling him to walk a road of faith right up to and through death. So my prayers were for abundant grace for all of us, most of all for Al. But if God gave others the faith to pray boldly for healing, that was fine with me. I was all for it!

A friend urged Al to travel to a faith healing meeting in another part of the country. Al did pray about it, but since he was not physically up to the trip, and since lots of people were already praying for him to be healed, he concluded that if the Lord chose to heal him, he could do it anywhere. Numerous other friends offered advice and products that had helped them or that were reputed to heal cancer. We were grateful for the love, concern, and kindness that prompted such offers. Had there been just one, we might have pursued it. But there were so many that the options were overwhelming. We didn't feel guilty about not trying them all. If Al's cancer had not been terminal, if we had had hope that he might survive, we might have struggled with guilt at not turning over every stone that presented itself. Even in that situation there would have been a limit to how many we could have tried. Ultimately, we all have to rest in God's providential care—to lead us to the right option, to heal us without it, or to call us home.

Al knew that God could heal him if he chose to, apart from the clinical trial or anything else. So he lived with the tension between wishing to remain in this life and accepting that he likely would not. In March he wrote an interesting post* that flowed out of that tension.

Like many of you, I have been flossing my teeth for years, but I simply never really enjoyed flossing. Perhaps it's because I try to do it last thing of the day, at a time when I'm usually tired. Who knows? Not surprisingly, I was all over any excuse that gave flossing a pass

---

* Blog posts throughout have had minor grammatical edits but retain the original content.

for the evening. Most of the time, however, I had no excuse, so I dutifully flossed.

Lately it crossed my mind that flossing my teeth may not matter anymore. If I'm dying, what's the point? My teeth are in good shape. (One of God's providential blessings in my life is that I have never had a cavity.) Just think—going to bed without any pre-bedtime rigmarole. Bliss. But somehow I just couldn't do it. And it wasn't the guilt of abandoned habit or improper hygiene crying out to my conscience. Rather, I realized that I would be caving in (in a small way) to hopelessness. Flossing your teeth is hardly earth-shaking. But somehow not flossing my teeth felt like giving up. I don't know what God is going to do with this cancer. So many people are praying for me/us. God might choose to extend my life, even bring me healing for years to come. I have not given up hope, and I'm not going to start a slide down the slippery slope.

Guess what? Each night flossing my teeth has become an act of faith and hope! At least one point in every day I am reminded that until I draw my final breath, God is my hope. And he can do as he alone is able.

In truth, I still sometimes feel the bother of flossing on the occasional late night, but each time I come to that moment of flossing, I am reminded that I want to live and that God is a God in whose faithfulness I can trust. He may choose not to heal me, but my choice is to hope in him. If I die, my hope is in his resurrection. If I live, my hope is in Christ as well.

# 13

# Companions in the Valley

For years and years, starting even before we were married, Al read through the book of Psalms once a month—twelve times a year. He continued to do that while he was sick. He loved the Psalms and they became even more precious to him as he faced death. This chapter contains some of his reflections on Psalm 23.

"The LORD is my shepherd, I shall not want." I first heard these words when I was perhaps four years old, living in Bartlesville, Oklahoma. My maternal grandparents were visiting and my grandmother was helping me learn Psalm 23 by heart. I believe it is the first text I ever memorized. I can still recall the sunny room where she was reading to me and the feeling of accomplishment that I felt in learning the entire passage. The central part of the psalm, the part about walking through the valley of the shadow of death and fearing no evil for "Thou art with me," seemed pretty distant in that sunny room long ago. In fact, I hardly could have told you what death was. Notwithstanding, these words somehow comforted even then. Shadowy valleys of whatever were banished in the warm sunlight of the moment.

Fifty years later these words address me in a more immediate way. And I am learning something new about how the Lord walks with us through the valley of the shadow of death—he comforts me directly through his Spirit and his Word. But he also uses the visible expression of the body of Christ, his people, to put hands and feet on his love for us. The Lord walks with me and he brings his people to walk with me as well.

God has used each and every one of you to comfort, love, and encourage my family and me. You are the visible expression of the resurrected Christ expressing to me the love that has the power to raise the dead. I don't walk in the valley of the shadow of death alone. I walk with the Lord, and he has sent you, his people, to walk with me. I am sorry to have (unintentionally) invited you along on this journey. It is my fervent prayer at this time that all of you will see the Lord when you walk here and that you will have others who will walk along with you and comfort you as well.

# SPRING '06

# 14

## Trusting the Good Shepherd

During the spring of 2006, the Lord set up a special one-on-one tutoring program for me in which he was the tutor, and I was the student—just the two of us. He chose an unexpected location for our tutoring sessions: the dentist's chair. In this book about Al's cancer, it seems crazy to include anything as insignificant as my dental problem, and yet through an issue with my tooth, the Lord taught me some of the deepest, sweetest, and most fruitful things about himself—lessons that helped me on the bigger journey through Al's cancer.

One of my teeth had had a crack in it for years and then literally cracked apart, so on a Monday in late March I went in to have it crowned. It can be challenging to get my left jaw numb for several medical reasons, so I never know whether the anesthetic will work or not. Our dentist, Dr. Cacovean, is a superb practitioner and also a wonderful woman, with the legendary patience of Job. When I have to have dental work done, she hangs in there with me and doggedly tries to subdue my uncooperative nerves. But that day, after three hours and the maximum number of allowable shots of two different kinds of anesthetic, when she had missed her lunch and who knows what else, the necessary nerves were still not numb enough to allow drilling. I remember sitting in the chair after each shot, waiting and hoping for my lip to go numb, looking out the window and begging the Lord, "*Please*, let the anesthetic work this time! I know you can do that. Please will you?" But to no avail.

We delayed for two days.

On Wednesday, after almost as many shots, the lower left jaw remained stubbornly sensitive. I felt badly taking up valuable real estate in the dentist's chair, but Dr. Cacovean was as patient and encouraging as ever. We were going to try again on Friday but had to put it off because my jaw was too traumatized (and remained so for a month).

That gave me time to contemplate. I thought maybe the reason Monday had failed was that I had not asked people to pray. So I asked friends to pray for my appointment on Wednesday, and I was confident that, once people were praying for the situation, everything would go smoothly. Nope. Clearly the Lord had other plans.

He must have had to superintend many details to keep an excellent dentist from finding the right nerve on so many tries over two days! But why? What was he up to? It had to be related to the challenge of Al's melanoma. Both had the feel of one option seeming to be the obvious best outcome (my jaw to go numb, Al not to have terminal cancer), and yet the Lord was choosing what seemed to be the less optimal path. Of course, he was 100 percent able to choose and accomplish my numbing and Al's healing. There was no question about either of those things and we continued to ask him to do both. But he was choosing a different outcome. *Why?*

In the case of Al's cancer, the whole thing seemed so big, so beyond us, and so mysterious that it was almost easier to think, *Well, God's ways are higher than ours, and he knows how to bring great good and blessing and glory out of very hard things, so we'll just walk with him and see how he does that in this situation.* On the other hand, my stubborn tooth was such an insignificant, mundane thing that it didn't necessarily occur to me to think of it in the same category. Yet there I was on Wednesday, wondering why the Lord would bother to hide my nerve from the needle rather than let the tooth get uneventfully crowned and forgotten about. That would have made so much more sense to me. After all, we had plenty going on right then, and lots of other things to think about and spend our time on besides me sitting in the dentist's chair for hours, over and over.

And that began to be a clue. "Too many things to do and think about." "Too many other things to spend our time on." Hmmm . . .

What I sensed about the question was that I was busy doing the having-a-sick-husband thing. I was busy figuring out what that looked like, how I could love Al best right then, how I could process it all in faith, how I could help the kids process it in faith, what I could do to get us all through it, etc. I was busy doing. I'm a doer.

There is nothing inherently wrong with being a doer. That's the way God made some of us, and that's fine. But each strength has a potential weakness, and in that particular case it was easy to depend on myself and forget to depend on God. It was so easy for me to get busy doing what I thought I needed to do (often perfectly good things that God did in fact want me to do) and forget what was more important.

The whole journey is supposed to be about growing to know God better. I don't mean just that the tooth crowning was about that—or even Al's cancer. *Life* is about that. The amazing God who made the universe is willing, even eager, to let us know him personally, intimately. Since we are blind and uninterested in that most of the time, he goes out of his way (and nudges us out of ours) to encourage us to get to know him. Sometimes it takes more than nudging to get our attention.

That week as I asked the Lord, "Why don't you want my tooth to be numbed and crowned so I can get on with life?" I realized that I had to kneel before him as Lord, King, and Master who called the shots and ordered our days, who knew what was *really* best for us. Eventually I ended up just kneeling quietly at his feet. He really was the shepherd, my shepherd, the Good Shepherd, who knew where the quiet waters and the green pastures were and who led me there. He was the LORD, and I could be genuinely content in his care and his sovereignty. If suffering came, it was under his care and direction, and therefore I could trust him to see me through it and to bring good from it. His choices of pasture might not always make sense to me. Other choices might have seemed more practical, sensible, fruitful, or beneficial. But he was the Lord. It was his job to choose the way, and mine to follow. In surrendering control there was such peace. In that quiet, still place at his feet, resting in the care of my Father and shepherd and trusting him, was perfect peace that passed understanding.

My jaw was still sore but the fruit of the dental ordeal was sweet. It was good of God to remind me who he was—my Lord and my shepherd—and who I was—his subject, his sheep, and his child. It was good to be reminded how much he loved me and that he would guide me and take care of me. I had a hunch that all those reminders were going to be very helpful in the months ahead. I did not always live in that place of trust—before, during, or after Al's illness. I often got distracted and busy and forgot about it. But I did live there more during that time than at any other period of my life, and that was precious.

# 15

## God with Us

Here is another bit of fruit from Al's reflection on the Psalms. He chose part of this verse to be the title of our blog: "God's Unfailing Love Endures Forever."

> The LORD will fulfill his purpose for me;
> your steadfast love, O LORD, endures forever.
> Do not forsake the work of your hands. (Psalm 138:8)

My friend David Powlison says that it is the King of the universe who leads us into fiery trials with the purpose of meeting us there. His leading is not without love and purpose. God is Father as well as King. In all that he does, he always acts with gracious and loving purposefulness. That includes suffering. He leads us into suffering, even through the valley of the shadow of death, for his purpose in our lives—a kind, gracious, and high purpose. God, the Father, meets us in our suffering. God, the Son, comes alongside us as fellow sufferer, One who has faced death and defeated it. God, the Spirit, fills us with the power that raised Jesus from the dead and reminds us of the glorious inheritance we have in Christ. God addresses our hearts and draws us to himself.

Psalm 138:8 has been a great encouragement about God's grace in my life (and every life). He will fulfill his purpose for me precisely because his faithful love endures forever.

God can heal. God ALONE heals. He will choose what he will do for his gracious purpose. As a sufferer once told Jesus, "If you are willing, you can heal me." There is no question that God *can* heal me, but I can't presume that he will *choose* to. I do know that he will do what he knows is best out of his faithful love. (The song "Blessed Be Your Name," by Matt Redman, has been significant for us in this context.)

Pray for healing. Pray boldly for complete healing, for his glory. Pray that I will trust him in his wisdom in whatever he chooses to do. Pray most of all that I can glorify God in this time. Pray Psalm 138:8 with us.

The Roman centurion who came to Jesus to ask him for healing for his servant did not ask Jesus to come under his roof, but only to speak the word. This example of faith has guided me: the people of God are praying for me; Jesus can respond and speak a word from heaven and I will be healed, by whatever means he chooses, medical or otherwise. In his wisdom and mercy, he may choose otherwise for his purpose and glory. I accept this.

It is not being healed from cancer in this life in which I ultimately hope. Rather, it is in Christ now and forever that I find my hope. I have been healed and raised in that ultimate sense by all that Christ has done. Blessed be the name of the Lord.

# 16

# Walking Blindfolded

My tooth still needed a crown, but we had to keep putting the dental work off because my jaw was so stiff and sore that I couldn't open it properly, even to eat. It was a month before we could try again. This time, on the fifth shot the area got decently close to numb. I still had sensation in the tooth, but it was pain I could live with, so we went ahead. I was pretty nervous when Dr. Cacovean started drilling without it being 100 percent numb, but it ended up being okay, and finally the job was done!

I started thinking about it. The previous summer when I had another tooth crowned, the jaw had gotten fully numbed and I remember vividly the exquisite sensation of non-feeling, knowing I could just relax and lean on that cushion of numbness that would protect me from pain. It struck me that this time we had to proceed without knowing whether or not, or to what degree, the pain would be there. I couldn't necessarily count on the protective cushion of Novocain.

During the spring of 2006, it seemed that the Lord had been calling me to walk in lots of uncertain situations (that felt similar to not knowing whether I would be numb during the dental procedure). Not knowing what would lie ahead with Al's cancer and what exactly we would have to go through. Sticking with the seminary course I was in that semester, having to take it one week at a time, not knowing whether I would be able to finish it or not. Wondering what life would look like when Al was not here anymore. Would I finish my degree at WTS? Would I find a job right away? Which job?

Those were uncomfortable lessons in living one day at a time and trusting things to the Lord. I would have preferred to know exactly what hard things lay ahead so that I could prepare for them. I like to plan ahead and prepare—preferably, even over-prepare—for unknowns in the future. But the Lord was setting my path through lots of unknowns that would probably include painful things, and all he would let me know ahead of time was that he would be right there with me as I walked that path. And that was enough. It was not the "enough" I might have thought I needed, but it was enough in his economy, his way of doing things, his love. Which meant it was definitely enough.

I would rather have had the comfortable assurance that I wasn't going to feel a thing under the dentist's drill. And I would rather have known that whatever lay ahead wouldn't really be too agonizingly painful. But the Lord knew better. If I had known all those things ahead of time, then I wouldn't have needed to trust him or depend on him so much. And while I might have preferred that, it would have been my great loss.

He is gracious to lead us through hard places where we have no other options but to put our shaky little hand in his and hold on tight, knowing that there may be scary things on the road but that he'll guide us safely and protect us well. Having no other choice enabled me to do just that. And he was there, holding on even more tightly to *my* hand.

# 17

# A New Normal

The spring rolled on. The kids were busy with the full schedules of their junior high lives. We had many lovely contacts and visits from friends, local and far-flung. I was still in my master's program at Westminster, so I tried to finish up the course I was taking and keep life running at home. Al dealt with pain and severe exhaustion and tried to chip away at two books he was under contract to write. He was on chemotherapy and still in the clinical medical trial, going on and off the targeted molecular therapy at different doses under Dr. Schuchter's supervision, in the hopes of minimizing the blisters and other side effects. We again asked him about dropping out of the trial, but he wanted to stick with it.

On one trip back from an appointment downtown, we ran into a friend on the train who also works in the field of biblical studies. He asked about a scholarly project Al was editing—this generation's edition of the Hebrew Bible, *Biblia Hebraica Quinta*. He inquired when it might be published. Publishing often runs behind projected completion dates, and part of Al's reply was to recount a story of the editors joking together, "By the time *BHQ* is finished, we will probably all have daggers by our names!" (A dagger indicates that the author, contributor, or editor died before the work was published.) The friend laughed at the story, which was Al's intention, but I noticed the tiniest wistful look around Al's eyes as he thought about the fact that he would not see *BHQ*'s completion and that his name would indeed be followed by a dagger.

It's curious the odd little things that apparently cross one's mind as death approaches. Al regretted that he would not get to find out how the Harry Potter series would end. He discovered the first book at the time it was published and introduced Eowyn and Alden to it even before it became a phenomenon. The four of us read most of the stories out loud together. Al also wished he could see how a nearby highway, Route 309, which had been under construction for years and years, would look when it was completed. (We actually detoured one day in order to drive on a newly finished interchange.)

We were all accustomed to Al being exhausted because of his fibro-myalgia, so in some ways life seemed somewhat normal. We still some-times talked with the kids about the cancer, about its effects, about Al dying, about heaven, about how God would see us through it all. It was always there in the background, but things had settled into a new "normal." Al wrote the following in May:

> We have settled into the middle part of the race. Most days now seem ordinary. We can sometimes almost forget that cancer is there lurking somewhere. Cancer has not meant that the Lord has let up on me in the pruning process. I am finding that the Lord continues to deal with my heart issues—unkindness, believing less than the best, etc. The good news is that God leads me into repentance. It's just that I seem to need to be repenting all the time these days! [Al was frustrated in his efforts to intervene in a conflict between friends and it took its toll on him.] I have been reading the Psalms most mornings. God uses them to speak to my soul and keep me sane.

# 18

# A Delayed Answer

Before the melanoma diagnosis, Al agreed to give the opening and closing lectures in a spring semester class he had previously taught for many years. In January I wondered whether he would still be here to give those closing lectures, but he was able to do it and it was a great joy to him.

As Al studied in the books of Ezra and Nehemiah for the closing lecture of that Westminster class in May, something struck him that encouraged him in our own situation. He wrote the following about it:

Nehemiah, who led Israel during the return from exile in Babylon, prayed a most amazing prayer recorded in the ninth chapter of the book of Nehemiah. After all that Israel had experienced in exile, and during a period when the rebuilding of Jerusalem hardly resembled the glory of Zion that Isaiah had spoken about, he remembered and praised God as an awesome God who created all things and who redeemed his people according to his covenant promise. He rehearsed Israel's history in his prayer—their covenant unfaithfulness and God's covenant faithfulness. He repeatedly mentioned and accented God's COMPASSION!

Nehemiah had seen judgment and oppression. He continued to see problems in the community of faith. Yet he extolled God for having compassion even when Israel behaved in the most depraved of ways toward him. He came to the end of his prayer crying out to the Lord, the Lord who had in compassion heard the groans of his people many times before. He cried out to say that God's people had become slaves in their own land! They had once experienced the miracle of deliverance from slavery in Egypt and settled in the land of Canaan, only to end up now as slaves in that land. His final word in the prayer: "We are in distress." A plea for help. There was still sin in the midst of the people. The reason for God to judge yet again was as great as it ever had been.

God answered that prayer with the greatest expression of compassion ever, although not in Nehemiah's lifetime. He sent a Deliverer who dealt with the sin in the midst of his people, a Deliverer who dealt with the real enemies: sin and death. In Christ, we see the answer to Nehemiah's prayer. No more threat of judgment because Christ has been judged in our place. God answered Nehemiah's prayer! But not in the way or the time frame in which he had almost certainly hoped.

I am in distress. But that is not the final word in my prayer. I live on the other side of the cross and the resurrection, that toward which Nehemiah looked from a distance. For me the final word is not distress, but hope in the One who has raised me from the dead and changed me into a new creature in Christ.

# 19

## Life Doesn't Slow Down

As I mentioned, there were three times that year when the pressures became too much. The most intense one was a two-day period late in May. As I reflected on why that weekend sent me over the top, I realized that it was partly because our ordinary life tended to be pretty full already. I looked back at my diary from that week, and although one of the days was blank, my diary reveals the activities from three of the four days leading up to that weekend.

In addition to the ordinary, routine tasks of life, plus trying to write two papers for my seminary class . . .

We had lovely visits with college friends who live out of state and with former seminary students from Scotland, England, and Puerto Rico.

I drove the kids to all their regular activities like piano lessons and band practices and went to Alden's track meet.

Eowyn and I talked through research for her science project, and Alden and I planned his upcoming thirteenth birthday party.

Our friend Erik came over to help us think about finances and the future, which was emotional.

Al and I had a difficult but helpful talk about the perennial challenges of working on writing projects together, a process that had been a point of tension in our relationship for years. We thought very differently about what was important to say, how to organize it, and how to communicate it clearly and effectively. Once, I spent hours helping him re-work an oral presentation only to hear him revert to the original without even realizing it. It was as if I'd never touched it. At that point

I threw up my hands in frustration and vowed that I was never going to write or edit with him again, though I later rescinded that decision. In the spring of 2006, Al was under contract to write two books, one on Judges and one on Isaiah. The talk we had that week encouraged me that we might be able to work together better. But the hope that flowed from that made the grief of losing Al all the keener, and the rest of the day tears were just below—or above—the surface. (In the end, the books never got finished.)

That week the young woman who was living with us found that some things were coming to a head in her life, so we had a lot of weighty things to talk through with her.

For some time there had been drama among Eowyn's friends such as I had never seen. The drain on some of the kids was enormous, affecting their sleep and schoolwork, driving them repeatedly to the guidance counselor's office for support. It was wreaking havoc within their group of friends. Eowyn, Al, and I had a lot of talks about it as we tried to help her navigate those waters.

I accompanied a friend to the police station to pick up the effects of his best friend, who had died tragically a few days earlier.

All this brings us to Friday.

# 20

# Flash Flood

Friday morning I picked Rebeckah up at the airport. She was in town for barely two days to be in the wedding party of a close high school friend, Lisa, and we were looking forward to seeing her. Lisa happened to also be the daughter of dear, longtime friends of ours. Al and her father Ed had worked out at the gym together two or three times a week for years. So we were doubly excited to see Becky *and* to celebrate with Lisa's family.

Al had been having increasing pain in his leg for a few days, so as soon as I returned from the airport, I took him to the doctor. An ultrasound confirmed a blood clot, and by midafternoon Al was admitted to the local hospital. After I had taken Eowyn and Alden to an orthodontist appointment and fed them supper, we trooped back to the hospital to visit him.

Al had had a Greenfield Filter inserted into his vena cava and, in typical Al fashion, he was captivated by the engineering ingenuity of the contraption. He showed us pictures and explained exactly how it worked. However, because he had to start blood thinners, he was stuck in the hospital for several days until they were regulated. The doctors absolutely would not let him out for any reason, so he was going to miss the wedding. *That* was devastating. I could see the keen disappointment and grief in his eyes.

Speaking of eyes, we had to fill out the standard hospital forms about risks, living wills, and organ donation. Usually those are just pro forma and you don't worry about actually dying, but in this case, it was a forceful, in-your-face reminder that Al *was* in fact dying, and that sometime in the months ahead he would not be needing his organs anymore. I am a firm believer in organ donation, but that day for some reason, the idea of someone else having Al's eyes was more than I could bear.

By this time I was feeling stretched thin, just trying to be in too many places at once. Having Al end up in the hospital was a monkey wrench. But I didn't have time to break down, or dwell on things, or sit down and have a good cry.

Al missing the wedding brought deep pain—for him, for Rebeckah, for Ed, and for me. I wondered how to get word to Rebeckah, who would be disappointed, and I wanted to try to encourage Al, but as I tried to think how, I found myself running out of emotional resources.

As we talked around Al's bed, we learned that there had been a truly awful new turn in the drama with Eowyn's friends, and she felt as if she were being fed into a wood chipper. She was in extreme distress. I was angry at the friend and felt overwhelmed at trying to help Eowyn deal with this new development when I was so short on both wisdom and emotional energy. I wasn't sure how much further we could stretch.

As Al and I were trying to help her sort through that, we got a call, out of the blue, from Alden's soccer coach. He said that their team was disbanding, effective that day, and if Alden wanted to play anywhere, he should call around in the next twenty-four hours to see if any teams were holding tryouts. How were we going to make all those calls with zero time available? But if we didn't, it might have a major impact on Alden's next year. Plus, we needed to help him sort through the emotions of this sudden surprise and why it happened, and think which teams we should call, what it would be like to try out against his former teammates, whether he should take a certain berth on a B team or put that at risk by waiting to try out for an A team, etc. Ordinarily we would all rally around to support him in such a situation and to help him figure it out, but that day there were just too many crises all at once. I was way, way beyond my resources to deal with them.

Of course, some of these problems are trivial next to the challenges people face in the Third World, but I still felt beaten up by their cumulative emotional impact. I felt weak and fragile. It was as if I had been sitting on a big rock in the middle of a stream when a flash flood hit and turned the stream deadly. Water was up to my neck, rushing past, occasionally whacking me with debris. But my back was pinned against the rock, and while the blows from the debris might hurt, I was not in danger of being swept away as long as my back was against the rock. I couldn't move out of the raging current; I couldn't so much as lift a limb to try, only face forward and take whatever came next. Yet because the rock wasn't going anywhere, neither was I. The Lord was that rock, and I knew that no matter how overwhelming the circumstances felt, he had hold of us, he would not let us go, and we would not be destroyed.

I'm so glad the Lord brought that image to my mind because that was only the beginning of tougher things ahead the next day.

# 21

# Turning an Unwelcome Corner

I slept badly that night. I woke up emotionally drained and running on adrenaline. A friend from overseas dropped by, having no idea of recent developments in Al's health. It was wonderful to see her, even though it delayed my departure to the hospital. Alden had two friends over, the computer was acting up as Eowyn tried to work on her science project, and I couldn't figure out what to wear to the wedding, so by the time I got to the hospital to visit Al before the wedding, it was 12:30.

A lot had happened. For one thing, Al had had a scan to make sure it was okay to administer blood thinners. For another, the father of the bride himself had been to visit Al! Our friend Doug had been in to see Al as well, and he was there (thankfully) when the report from the scan came back, stating that there was swelling in Al's brain.

Oh . . .

That signified a lot of things. It meant, presumably, that the melanoma had spread to the brain. If so, that meant the end of PFS—progression-free survival. Either the clinical trial had never made a difference at all or it had worked briefly and then ceased to be effective. Either way, he was automatically out of the trial. And either way it meant that the cancer was active, and we were now verifiably on the downhill slope toward the end.

More disheartening was the fact that every medical person who came into the room asked, "Have you noticed any personality changes?" Our hearts sank at that. The tumor was in the lobe of the brain that affects personality, and the implication was that if things went badly,

Al could become someone different than he had always been—perhaps short-tempered, or mean, or inappropriate. That was a terrible thought for both of us. I could see that that *really* distressed him. He told me, "I can face a lot of things, but I really don't want to become someone else and have our kids remember me that way. That's hard."

However, there was a slice of good news. The mass in the brain also meant that they could not administer blood thinners, so there was no reason to keep Al in the hospital. He could be released and go to the wedding after all! Amid everything, Al was elated about that.

We went home and got a wheelchair. Al put on a suit, and off to the wedding we went, with such mixed emotions that I don't think we knew which end was up. But we *were* thankful to be going to the wedding together.

# 22

# Torn Down the Middle

The ceremony was beautiful. Lisa was beautiful. Rebeckah was beautiful. Ed and Sheri were beaming, and we were very grateful to be there.

As Rebeckah walked down the aisle as a bridesmaid, we could not help thinking ahead to the day when she would walk down the aisle as a bride and Al would not be there to escort her. As Ed and Lisa came down the aisle, we felt *such* great joy for them in this wonderful day. And at the same time we felt such a stabbing, heartrending grief that Al and Rebeckah would never get to share such a moment. We didn't need to say that out loud. We each knew what the other was thinking, and we just squeezed hands and cried through our smiles. I always cry at weddings, but at this one I thought I would never turn off the tears.

Afterward, when Ed saw Al in the receiving line, the two of them hugged each other for a long time and just bawled.

Al managed his severe pain through most of the reception. There came another moment that was as agonizingly bittersweet as the walk down the aisle: the father-daughter dance. Again, we were thrilled for Ed and Lisa, even as we ached for the future day when Rebeckah would have no father to dance with her. She stood behind him in his wheelchair, with her hand on his shoulder and his hand over hers, and they both wept for joy and sadness.

When the general dancing started, the three of us slipped out to the lobby. We told Becky the news about the brain tumor and cried together. Al said through his tears, "I don't know how these things work, whether people in heaven can see what goes on here on earth or not. But if so, I will see you on your wedding day, and I will rejoice with you. And even if it doesn't work that way, God will be your father on that day."

# 23

# Father of the (Someday) Bride

Here is Al's version of that wedding weekend.

In May, Becky, my oldest daughter, came home for thirty-six hours in a weekend to be in the wedding of her dear friend, Lisa Welch. On the Friday before the wedding on Saturday, I was admitted to the hospital with a very painful blood clot in my right leg. Because it would take at least three days in the hospital to be sure that the medication for thinning my blood was properly regulated, I would not be able to attend the wedding. Nor, as a result, would I see my daughter. I had been in either the emergency room or the hospital since she arrived and she had wedding-related activities in the evening on Friday. She would have the wedding on Saturday and then catch a 7 a.m. flight Sunday. This was all disappointing, to say the least.

Add to this that the father of the bride, Ed Welch, is one of my dearest friends. For years we have gone to the gym together twice a week. We may not exercise the major muscle groups, but we do give our jaw muscles a real workout. Ed also teaches at Westminster, and we attended the same church where we were elders together. So, not only was I going to miss seeing my daughter at the wedding, I was going to miss celebrating with Ed. The doctors were firm about my situation: my clots must be brought under control, and that would require constant supervision in the hospital for the next three days. No way was I going to get a furlough to attend this wedding, which was a crushing blow.

Saturday morning, the day of the wedding, who showed up at my bedside, but Ed, the father of the bride! With so many other things on the mind of the father of the bride and so many other things to be doing, there he was visiting me. I was deeply touched. We talked about all manner of things, especially the wedding and the joy this wedding was bringing to our church community, shown by how many had pitched in to help and had given of their time to make this a wonderful celebration. Apparently the church was swimming in flower arrangements prepared with love by a friend of the family. Everything was in place and ready to go. I was moved to tears for joy at such kindness and beauty, and I wept at the prospect of missing the event.

After Ed left, I received the surprising news that I could go home after all! (It was actually bad news that made it possible for me to escape: a tumor in my brain had been discovered, which meant that I could not receive blood thinners and the hospital therefore had no reason to keep me.) It was a gift in disguise that I could now attend the wedding to see my daughter and to celebrate with the Welches. Being released from the hospital had the downside that the excruciating pain caused by the clot was undiminished and untreated, but I was going to the wedding.

And the wedding was certainly one of the loveliest I have ever attended. The joy of seeing Ed and his daughter come down the aisle and to share in the joy of that moment was worth the pain of sitting in the pew (I was able to keep my foot elevated, so it was mostly manageable). And seeing my own beautiful daughter come down the aisle as a bridesmaid was like a little glimpse of a day in the future: Becky walking down an aisle as a bride.

We went for a bit of the reception, enough to see the father of the bride dance with his daughter. It was at this point that Becky came over and put her arms on my shoulders and rested her chin on my head and we wept together. Joy and grief mixed together. Without having to speak, we knew that we were given the gift of enjoying vicariously through Ed and Lisa that which we were not likely to experience ourselves: father and daughter dancing at her wedding. We went outside and Libbie joined us. Weeping for joy at this day and grieving for the day that we would likely not have. All I could say was that we must trust and believe that God will be

Becky's father on that day and that we don't know how that can be now, but that he is kind and gracious and will meet her.

It was a day of a gift from God—the joy of our dear friends spilled over on us to bless us; against hope I was able to be there; the future that my daughter and I will likely not share we nonetheless enjoyed for a moment through our friends. Even the grief was a gift because we had it together and it rested in the love and blessing that we enjoy now.

I have another daughter, Eowyn. In February, two days after the tumors in my lungs were definitively diagnosed as melanoma, she and I had gone out to dinner alone and wept over the same issue. She had said, "Dad, there are many hard things, but one of the hardest is that you might not be there for my wedding." We both wept. For both of my daughters this had been very much in my mind. And it was very much in theirs as well.

And I have a son, Alden, for whom the same issue will arise. While he and I have not spoken about it (it tends to be more on the minds of fathers and daughters perhaps), it is still an issue of the heart.

God works in ways I don't understand. We see his goodness. And sometimes we simply look and see him, without knowing anything more than that he is near and cares.

I think that last paragraph might be my favorite thing that Al ever wrote.

# 24

# When Sorrow Deepens Joy

Five days after Lisa's wedding was Westminster's graduation. When we thought Al was going to start blood thinners, it looked as if he might not be able to attend graduation, and that was a sore disappointment to him, knowing it would be his last. As Academic Dean, Al read the names of the graduates as they received their diplomas, and it happened to also be his turn that year to give the charge to them. He was *so* looking forward to it. Here is some of what he wrote about it afterward:

> Today Westminster Seminary graduated more than 125 students . . . I was thrilled simply to be there and to be part of the ceremony.
>
> One of my tasks was to read the name of each of the graduates as they walked across the stage to receive their diploma. There really is nothing more thrilling than to see the success of your students. Students probably don't realize how precious they become to their teachers through the years. What a bittersweet process teaching can be—forging strong bonds and relationships with students, knowing full well that in a few very short years we will be sending them out of our lives. Perhaps forever. It's like raising children, only on a much shorter time cycle.
>
> For me today was special because I had the opportunity to give the charge to the graduates. Again, I cannot say enough how grateful I was to the Lord to be able to do it—even having to sit on a stool, with my clotted leg propped up. Sort of like having a fireside chat in the den or something. I was grateful that the Lord kept the pain in my leg at manageable levels. And the help from so many was just overwhelming. The president even wheeled me down the aisle and up onto the stage.

Afterward I had wonderful conversations with graduates and alumni and parents. Gift upon gift for me . . . Just wanted to share the joy of the day, undimmed by other circumstances in my life. In fact, other circumstances added something to the joy of the day! God is good.

Everybody knew this would be Al's last graduation. I sat in the back with my friend Sheri and bawled, anticipating that a day would come when Alasdair and I would cross that stage and Al would not be there to see it.

# SUMMER '06

# 25

## "Rumpled of Spirit"

Not surprisingly, during that period Al struggled with his emotions. "Feeling rumpled of spirit" is how he described it.

Like a seesaw, my emotions have been up and down from day to day lately. Yesterday was a particularly "blue" day, perhaps one of the more depressed days I have had in years. Today started similarly as well.

There are many potential factors, physical and emotional: Two decades of increasing fibromyalgia pain and exhaustion have been continual companions, which cancer has not managed to frighten away. Now stir in heat, pain from the blood clot in my leg, lack of exercise, headaches from swelling in my brain, the impact of various drugs I have been on for treatment, and the steroids I'm currently taking for swelling around the brain tumor, all impacting rest and sleep. Lack of energy and pain make sitting at the computer for any stretch of time a problem. (I don't use the computer simply for writing, but I use it very much as a help for my devotions and study of the Scriptures.) What little energy I have has sometimes gone into organizing medical treatments and procedures, etc. (And Libbie does so much here as well!) Season all this with a tumor in the brain signaling that the advance of the cancer continues, and there seem to be any number of reasons for what I have been feeling.

Yesterday was a day where it was hard not to treat my feelings, whatever their source, as the ultimate reality in life. Reading a simple book about a simple truth (known from the beginning of my Christian life) reminded me that I don't look inside for help,

but to the Lord, through his Spirit in his Word for the truth. That
truth comes from what Christ has done for me in his death and
resurrection.

In particular, the chapter I was reading was one on listening
to the Scriptures, to the truth that comes from God, not to my
feelings. My feelings are not good and wise authorities, but are
often led by other circumstances. Bringing my heart and thoughts
captive to Christ, to the living Lord, began to change my heart.
It comes from outside in. God used the words of several of you
through email and in person to point me to God's personal care
and love.

A good reminder that our emotions don't determine reality; only
the Lord does.

# 26

# What We Don't Deserve

Al was always kind, welcoming, and patient through all the years I knew him. I think a large part of the reason was his deep awareness of God's grace. He had experienced the Lord's mercy and compassion, and he extended it to others.

Among the Psalms, he had always been drawn to the collection attributed to the Sons of Korah. During the year he was dying, he came to understand and appreciate them more than ever. Here are some reflections he wrote.

Psalm 42

I have always been deeply touched by this first psalm of the Sons of Korah. Shaking his head at himself and exhorting his own soul to look beyond his feelings to his Savior and his God (42:5, 11), the psalmist shows simple faith in the power of God's presence and the grace that comes from that presence.

Eleven psalms are attributed to the Sons of Korah. They breathe a deep passion for being near the Lord and his presence. They lament being separated for any reason. When in despair, the Sons of Korah exhorted their own souls to remember the goodness and grace they had received, and that they would again experience joy and worship in his presence.

So who were the Sons of Korah? And who was Korah, their ancestor? Korah was a Levitical priest but also a leader of a rebellion against Moses and Aaron (see Numbers 16). He and his family were swallowed by the earth, however "the line of Korah did not die out" (Numbers 26:11 NIV).

Theirs was a family with shame attached to their name, perhaps forever. What hope had this family of honor, much less of service in the house of the Lord, in the very PRESENCE of the Lord? Incredibly, we see this family now emerging as ministers in the house of the Lord, as ones from whom glorious psalms of praise to God come. What happened?

Grace. Concrete and coming from restoration to the presence of God. King David was God's human vessel to show grace to this family of priests by making them gatekeepers and ministers for the temple that his son Solomon would build. David himself had seen grace from God given to his own family (his ancestresses Rahab and Ruth were Gentiles, impossibly included in the people of God by God himself). God, through David, invited the descendants of Korah back into ministry, into his very presence! God not only took away their shame but restored their honor by putting them near his presence. This is not just abstract kindness, but living, ongoing relationship with the holy God who had judged their forebears. How much greater is the grace we have received in Christ—brought near to his presence forever. We have hope where there was no reason to have any hope. How great is our God!

As I said, eleven psalms of passion for God's presence are attributed to the Sons of Korah. They look beyond themselves for a hope that was not theirs by nature or right. They look to the One who lifted them up, dead dogs by all circumstances, now gatekeepers and ministers in the presence of the Lord.

What a picture of the grace that comes from God. Nothing they did brought this on them. God, through David, acted to bring them life, and they responded with dedicated worship and songs of praise that minister to you and me three millennia later.

# 27

# Making the Best of the Situation

In the aftermath of the wedding and graduation whirlwind, it was decided that Al would undergo gamma knife treatment rather than brain surgery. The gamma knife uses dozens of high-power radiation beams coming from all directions around the head, all directed at a single spot in the brain so that the spot gets zapped, but the rest of the brain tissue receives much less radiation. We were thankful that such a thing had been developed so that Al didn't have to go through a full craniotomy.

Because we had to report to Pennsylvania Hospital downtown by 6 a.m., we decided to make the best of the situation and take advantage of the opportunity to stay at a quaint little bed and breakfast a few blocks away the night before. Friends helped by staying at our house with Eowyn and Alden, so we ended up having a lovely, relaxed time together, just the two of us. We even went to an Indonesian restaurant that brought back memories of wonderful dinners with friends when we lived in Amsterdam, while Al was working on his PhD. One of those dinners had been in celebration of Al's fiftieth birthday. It was odd to think that just three-and-a-half years later, he was undergoing treatment for cancer that was going to cut his life short.

The concentrated dose of radiation left Al a bit weak and wobbly for quite a while, but it was still a blessing to have dodged full-out brain surgery. Best of all, it meant he would be able to go to Rebeckah's graduation from college in New Hampshire.

# 28

# A Proud Dad's Last Graduation

Rebeckah graduated in June, and we were *all* there, even Al. Back in January I had wondered whether Al would even be alive in June, much less able to travel, but there he was at her graduation. It meant so much to him and to her. We knew he would miss Eowyn and Alden's graduations—from high school and college—but at least he was there for Rebeckah's.

It was a day of all kinds of joy. We were so proud of Becky! Our niece and nephew-in-law came too, and we discovered they were expecting. Professor Rassias, who had been special to Al and to me, as well as to Alasdair and Rebeckah, was there, and we got to see him and his wife Mary. Becky's improv comedy troupe did one last show, which was such fun. The weekend was full of laughter and happiness (and a few tears) all around.

Afterward we helped Rebeckah move out of her apartment. It was hard for Al to just lie on the couch and watch without being able to pitch in, but at least he was there and part of the fun and the chaos.

Originally Rebeckah and some of her friends had talked about moving to Colorado or someplace, getting jobs, and settling in an area that was new to all of them. But once Al got sick, she definitely wanted to be back in Philly to have as much time with him as possible. She and one of her college roommates rented an apartment in our town and figured they would sleep on the floor until they could acquire furniture. But the week before she moved in, we received an email: "Student dorm closing. All furniture free." The Lord furnished their entire apartment in a matter of hours.

Alasdair and his wife Lauren moved to Philly the same weekend, so in the space of about forty-eight hours, we suddenly had the whole family—plus college roommates—back in town. It was heavenly! From then on, we all got together every Sunday afternoon, and we had lots of contact individually beyond that. What a priceless gift!

I have thought since high school, when one of my college-age friends lost his dad, that it must be incredibly difficult for a child to be away at college when a loved one dies. The child wants to be home with the loved one for however much time is left, long or short, but that may not coincide with college semesters. And afterward, how can he/she concentrate on coursework? I was grateful that the Lord timed Al's death between Rebeckah finishing college and Eowyn starting, and I pray that he will sustain kids who do find themselves in that situation.

# 29

## It's Not Up to Me

In June I was feeling particularly stressed by the weight of present life details and anxious about future ones. I think most of all I was fretting about the prospect of becoming a single parent and feeling decidedly unequal to that task. There were *so* many things that Al did wonderfully with our kids that I did not. He was so intentional. Every Saturday for years and years he took one of them out to Rocky's Deli for lunch to have one-on-one time and to talk about whatever they wanted to. He coached their teams when his health allowed. He read the books they were reading so they could talk about them. He asked probing questions and really wanted to know what they were thinking. He understood Rebeckah's fears and Eowyn's objections at hard theological questions. He was *always* willing, at the drop of a hat, to talk, to process things, to encourage.

I was none of those things. The thought of being the sole parent in the near future was daunting and scary, and I was definitely worrying about it and letting it get to me. In the space of two days, Al and one of the kids each asked, "Are you okay? You seem really frazzled."

I admitted to feeling frazzled, but I think I chalked it up to the current press of responsibilities. I don't think I admitted to Al that I was worrying about the future. Maybe that was because I knew it would distress him to think that I was worrying about him not being around. There was nothing he could do about that, after all, and I thought it would make him feel bad. Or maybe it was because that unknown future was something I was going to have to handle on my own, without him, and I was already starting to try to handle it myself. Either way, it was a bad call to keep it from him. He would have pointed me to the Lord and helped me put my confidence and trust there.

During this time, it became clear that my tooth was not quite fixed. It seemed there was a crack in the root underneath the crown, so once again I was back in the dentist's chair. I remembered vividly how in April the Lord had shepherded me into the place of trusting his good plan and resting in his care for me, which is the only place of real peace. So that is where I wanted my mind and heart to be for the upcoming appointment. Instead, I was terribly distracted and out of sorts.

I figured, *Oh great. If the Lord found it necessary in April to extend the process of getting my jaw numb to remind me to rest in his care, then I am really in for it this time.* Yet the Novocain worked on the very first shot! Not only that, Dr. Cacovean was able to do a root canal that would solve the problem altogether. Go figure.

So I did go figure. And I remembered something I had known for years and years: It's not about *me* getting *my* heart right so that God can work. I cannot determine a single outcome of anything God may do by my heart attitude or by anything else I do. I was reminded again that he is the Lord. He is sovereign and will do what he knows is best for his children. And while he does call us to give him our whole hearts in glad surrender at every moment, his love and care for us don't depend on how well or poorly we do that.

That is exactly what I needed to be reminded of right then. As I worried about the future and how I would handle important things that I often do poorly and that Al did well, I needed to remember that the Lord would be there. He was not bound by my failures. I fail, but Jesus doesn't, and that is what God's love for me—and for our children—is based on. He could guide the dentist's needle and fix my recalcitrant tooth despite my lack of faith, and he could and would take care of us all in the future, even in the areas where I was weak.

Al would have told me that, if I'd let him in on what was bothering me. But the Lord was gracious to bring me to that place by his Spirit.

Looking back on it, I marvel at how perfectly the Lord used something as small as a bad tooth to remind me of exactly what I needed to remember about him in each different moment. Each lesson, from a different angle, was a tender reminder from my heavenly Father of his steadfast, faithful care for me.

# 30

## Giving In? Giving Up?

I think many people, especially those with health limitations, struggle with knowing when to push through pain and fatigue and when it's okay to make rest a priority. Al struggled with that for years because of his fibromyalgia, and all the more as cancer sapped his small reserves of strength. As he struggled with limited energy to tackle things he very much wanted to get done before he died, he wrote:

> During the last dozen years or so, I have lived with the perpetual pain, exhaustion, and brain fog of fibromyalgia. In that time I have felt constantly torn between the demand of my body for rest, and the demands of my job, family, church, etc., to carry out the responsibilities of life. I could never sleep deeply because of the 24/7 muscle pain, so day after day, year after year I became increasingly exhausted—sort of like experiencing a severe jet lag that never goes away. My body would incessantly scream for rest, but I set my jaw and "pushed through it" to do whatever it was that had to be done at that moment. When I could rest, it was rarely restorative, so I had to just keep going. Any time I "gave in" to the need to rest I felt guilty, thinking that I had too much to do to be resting, that people were counting on me to get X, Y, or Z done, or that I had committed to do X, Y, Z, or that I just wanted to help someone with X, Y, Z, and that my condition wasn't that bad, that I was just caving in to weakness. As levels of exhaustion escalated because I resisted rest and worked instead, the desire for rest became more global and the overwhelming drive to give in to it made me feel even guiltier, as if I were being tempted to give up altogether.

Now that I find myself in a situation of being weaker than ever and seeming to need to rest a majority of the time, I'm not sure what to do with my sense of guilt. Am I "giving in" when I rest so much? Am I "giving up"? Is there a difference between those two? Is it okay to rest most of the time because my body needs that, and I don't have much choice, and that's really okay? Or does that equal "giving up," and I should still operate in a mode of always trying to push through the fatigue? Having longed for rest for so many years and having felt that I should resist that longing, now that I am more tired than ever, I find my body and soul often longing for that Eternal Rest that we look forward to in Christ. Is that giving up? Or is it like what Paul said, "For me to live is Christ and to die is gain"? Was guilt genuine and appropriate before cancer but no longer? Or was it wrongly placed even before?

I don't want to give in to laziness, or self-indulgence, or shirking tasks the Lord has given me to do. And I don't want to give up on life while the Lord still gives me life to live. Where guilt is real, I want to repent and receive the Lord's forgiveness. At this point I am trying to sort out the correct and faith-filled balance between working through the pain and fatigue and taking time to rest.

In whatever time the Lord gives me, I have to choose very carefully what to do with my reduced energy and waking hours. Of course I want to spend time with my family most of all. Beyond that, there are unfinished tasks I believe the Lord wants me to complete. With only an hour or so per day when I can think clearly enough to work on those—two hours on a good day—they are progressing slowly. Writing clearly has always been a struggle for me, and as my concentration wanes it is more difficult than ever. Please pray for wisdom to know how to prioritize and use my time.

In response to Al's wrestling, my sister, who also struggles with fibromyalgia and who is wise, pointed out that in John 4, the reason Jesus had his famous conversation with the woman at the well was that he was *tired* and *needed to sit down and rest*. As she said, if he had pushed on rather than stopping when he needed to, he would not have had that conversation, and think what we would all have lost! His talking to the woman was exactly what his Father had planned, and it happened because Jesus stopped to rest.

# 31

## A Table Before Me

That summer, even though Al was weak from cancer, fibromyalgia, steroids, and radiation, we were able to travel a bit. Al was keen to go to his high school reunion in South Dakota, and his health held up for that. He was so excited to see his old friends again.

A family we knew from Alden's soccer team loaned us their house at the New Jersey shore for a weekend, and our family of nine (Al and I, Alasdair and his wife Lauren and housemate/former college roommate Andy, Rebeckah and her roommate Melissa, Eowyn and Alden) had a lovely weekend there. In the Lord's providence, Al's health and stamina improved a bit for those few days, which allowed him just enough strength to ride two or three waves. He could not have done that the week before or after.

Al would have loved to go back to Amsterdam one more time, and I regret that I didn't figure out a way to get him there. Whereas Al always dreamed big and made things happen, I tend to "think small" and give up too easily, and this may have been another example of that. I really don't know when or how we could have done it, but if I had worked harder on the idea, maybe it would have succeeded.

We went down to Florida to visit Al's family, which is always a treat, and never more so than then. However, one evening while we were there, Al had ferocious, debilitating headaches. It was hard to see him in pain and to see Al's mom watch him in pain. As a mother, I can imagine how hard it is to see your child suffer like that. It made my heart break to see her grief.

We all lived with a constant awareness that death was waiting in the wings to take Al. Every day we treasured the fact that he was still with us. The image of death hovering nearby made me think of Psalm 23:5, "You prepare a table before me in the presence of my enemies."

I pictured a group of people within sight of—who knows, maybe even surrounded by—enemies, sitting down and eating a meal at a table. That's bold. It's gutsy. It says to the enemies, "You are so little to be feared that we can sit down and have a nice meal *in your presence* and not be afraid." The Lord is so mighty, so far above all other gods, that he can set a table for his people right in front of their enemies and protect them in safety and peace while they feast. The enemies can't do anything about it but look on in frustration and shame. It flaunts the enemies' impotence. If VeggieTales were doing an animation of this scene, the growling, boasting enemies would suddenly doubt themselves and shrink to miniature size.

The Bible describes death as our ultimate enemy (Genesis 3:3; Isaiah 25:7–8; 1 Corinthians 15:55; Revelation 6:8; 20:13–14), but Jesus has defeated death. He broke its power over himself, and as he unites us to himself, its power over us is broken as well. We simply don't need to be afraid of death because for those in Christ, death is only the transition to a fantastic life with the Lord himself. It will be a life beyond the wildest kind of wonderful that our imaginations can dream up. Death, rather than being terrifying, has been robbed of its power, like the impotent enemies of Psalm 23. It really has lost its sting and been swallowed up in Jesus's victory (1 Corinthians 15:55).

We knew we were living in the presence of death. We were very aware that Al's days were numbered. (Of course all of our days are numbered, but we happened to know that, barring a miracle, the number of *his* days was few.) We did not deny or ignore that truth. But as we lived day by day, it didn't scare or intimidate us. Death was always there, waiting in the wings, slouching against the wall of our dining room as we ate dinner, a constant wannabe menace. But it had no power over us. Its teeth and claws had been removed. This is not to say that there was no grief as we contemplated life without Al. The grief was keen and the tears flowed freely, but we grieved with an absolutely real and concrete hope that he would be with Jesus in heaven, and that eventually we would join them there. That took the fear away. Like the author of Psalm 23, we feasted on the abundance our Shepherd provided and enjoyed it in peace and security even as our enemy, death, looked on impotently, unable to frighten us or make us despair. Our amazing, all-powerful Shepherd was with us, looked out for us, provided for us, guided us in his paths, and anointed our heads with the oil of his Spirit. We were confident that his goodness and mercy would be with us all the days of our lives, and we looked forward—Al sooner and the rest of us whenever—to dwelling with him in his house forever.

# 32

# A Daughter's Perspective

In July, Eowyn (then age fifteen) wrote the following on the blog:

All right, I'm writing because I have been informed that some people would be interested in knowing how the younger members of the Groves family are holding up with this situation God has put in our lives. So I (Eowyn) will try to put into words how life has been, and what I've been feeling.

We're all going to die someday. However, it still came as a shock when, back in January and February, we found out for sure that my dad is going to die. Over the past six months, I've been realizing that the day we will die doesn't change. My dad's cancer simply gives us a better idea as to when the Lord is going to take my dad to be with him. God is more powerful than the cancer. Though the cancer seems to be controlling my dad's ability to live, I take comfort in knowing that the cancer is just part of God's plan. Just like he also has a plan for you and for me.

The idea of losing my dad is something that's very hard for me. It hurts to think of life without my dad, and I am frequently emotional. However, I know that heaven is infinitely better than life here on Earth. I take comfort in the fact that when my dad is in heaven, he will be without suffering. My dad's going to be worshiping our God and King. Because the perishable will become imperishable, death has lost its sting; we look with longing toward eternity, which is symbolized by death. So as much as I wish my dad would live for the next forty years, I know I don't need to be sad by the prospect of death. I know it's going to be hard to live with a feeling of loss, but, thanks to Jesus, I know it's really going to be an unimaginable blessing for my dad.

On top of knowing that my dad will be enjoying life in heaven, I have the added comfort and joy of knowing that someday I'm going to join Jesus and my dad in heaven. Though I look ahead with premonition toward a great loss, I also look ahead with great joy and happiness for my dad in his home-to-be.

Instead of dwelling on the fact that the time I have left with my dad is short, God has been teaching me to be thankful for the blessing of the fifteen years God has put an amazing father in my life. I really couldn't ask for a better dad. My dad is loving and caring, but most importantly, he continually challenges me in my faith and points me to Christ. I truly don't know how I am going to get along without him, but I am trusting in God to take care of me, and to keep drawing me to him.

I still struggle somewhat with the idea of death, and the prospect of my dad's cancer, but in the end I know that God is sovereign, and that he loves me and will provide for my family. In all of this, my heart has really ached for people in our situation who don't know God, and who have no hope in the face of death.

I deeply appreciate everyone's prayers for my family and for me. I have really felt God's love through the body of Christ as they have surrounded us with love and prayers. My prayer is that God will bless you in your life as much as he's been blessing me, even in the midst of my dad's cancer.

# 33

## A Son's Perspective

Alden (then age thirteen) wrote the following:

Way back in January, I was told by my parents that my dad had gone for his routine X-ray and the doctor had found two "spots" on his lungs. Less than a month later we discovered, as we'd somewhat been expecting, that they were in fact melanoma. We gradually gained information about it, and I became more and more nervous about it. Normally I am not an emotional person and I'm pretty laid back, but my dad's whole situation really made me express some of my emotions. Often my emotions would stay pent up inside me, but sometimes I would let them out. My dad's always struggled with fibromyalgia, but it's still difficult to see him in pain so often.

One thing that's been tough is that most of my friends are not very clued in about his situation in general. My sister's friends have come alongside of her, and obviously my parents' friends are there as well, but I've somewhat struggled with not being able to talk with anyone. Thankfully, my parents sit down and talk with us often, and discuss how we're all feeling. Throughout this whole situation, God has shown me many things. One thing that is immediately apparent is just how important it is (and a blessing) to have parents who still love each other and are still married, and love us.

My dad always encourages me to have daily quiet times, but I always "forget." One day I realized that he is a wise man and decided to open up my Bible. That day I had been thinking about why God had picked my dad and our family to undergo this trial. I decided on James 1, and read it.

*"Count it all joy, my brothers, when you meet trials of various kinds, for you know that the testing of your faith produces steadfastness. And let steadfastness have its full effect, that you may be perfect and complete, lacking in nothing." (James 1:2–4)*

Wow, God spoke straight into my life that day! As he does so well in everyone's life, if you stop and take the time to listen. One of my good friends, Jesse, and I met together one day and prayed about all the things we could think of to pray for, and then took some time to pray with my sister and her friends concerning my dad's situation. One of my other friends on a junior high retreat told me that in a good way, my family was the best family she knew to go through this ordeal. Words and actions like these have really encouraged me to go on.

The song "Blessed Be Your Name" and the whole book of Job are real testimonies to our situation. One of the lines in the song says, "You give and take away, you give and take away, my heart will choose to say, 'Lord, blessed be your name.'" God gives and he takes away as he's showed us through our dad, but no matter I'm willing to bless the Lord's name.

My dad: one of the most caring, loving, strongest Christian guys I know. He has helped to mature me and raised me under the Lord. To me, my dad's as old as it gets, but in the overview, he's still young. I guess "only the good die young," right?? I love my dad so much, and it's really hard for me to think that in two years when I move up to the high school, he may not be there. But when I think of how much I love my dad, I know that God loves him so much more. God has a plan for all of us, so I know that even from the beginning it was the same, but it doesn't take away the sadness. In the words of my dad himself, it is not wrong to grieve; in fact it's good, but in Christ, we grieve with the hope of new life. I am not as eloquent of a writer as my sister, but I just wrote in to let y'all know what my deal is.

Let me add that it is hardly surprising if twelve-year-old boys are not skilled at knowing how to comfort a friend whose dad is dying! Skill sets are age-appropriate. Alden's friends are great guys who have loved him well.

# 34

## Just the Two of Us

In August, Eowyn and Alden were away at youth group camp for a few days, and we had a taste of what the empty nest years might have been like, when the kids would grow up, leave the house, and take all their hustle and bustle with them. It was sad to know that we would never share that experience. But the time together was a gift.

"What would you like to do tonight?"

"Well, we could keep reading *Gilead*. Or go to a movie."

"Are you sure you feel up to going out to a movie?"

"Hopefully. Would you enjoy that?"

"Of course. You know me—I'm always up for a movie. But not if it would wear you out."

"Well, let's see after I rest."

"Okay."

"I don't really care what we do. It's nice to just be together."

"I agree."

# 35

## Surgery

While the kids were away, Al had an MRI and a follow-up appointment with the doctor who had performed the gamma knife procedure in June. We thought it would be a routine visit, but we could tell that something was up. The doctor was trying to hide his astonishment that Al was able to be on his feet and function so well. Apparently the MRI showed that the tumor had doubled in size and that there were three new ones and a lot of swelling. The doctor's staff was incredibly efficient. Within hours, Al had tests, was admitted to the hospital, and was scheduled for brain surgery first thing the next morning!

Eowyn and Alden returned from camp to the shocking news. But we all went down to the hospital and had a great time around Al's bed.

The next day, during the surgery, one of our pastors and a good friend came down to encourage me. Then two of Al's colleagues came and stayed with me most of the day. That was such a blessing. Meanwhile, various people supported our kids, drove them where they needed to go, took them out for ice cream, etc.

The surgery went smoothly. The tumor was right on the surface of the brain in a very accessible spot, and the doctor was pleased with how things turned out. He even told me with a smile that he had carefully placed the scar behind Al's hairline for cosmetic purposes. How's that for thoughtfulness?

The hospital allowed us all to be with Al after the surgery. His head was wrapped in a bandage like a Sikh's turban. He looked as if he'd been in a war, but he was his true self.

At one point the ICU nurse was trying to undo a particularly tight connection in one of the tubing units and jokingly complained, "Who was the macho man in the OR who put this together? I'd like to give him trouble for it." Al, who was still groggy and in and out of wakefulness, managed to mumble through his oxygen tube and swollen lips, "His name is Mike."

The surprised nurse asked, "What's his last name?" Al didn't know, but he was able to tell her what area Mike lived in, and the name of the high school he had attended! I would never have thought to ask an OR nurse anesthetist his name, much less what high school he'd gone to. And I certainly wouldn't have remembered that information on the other side of brain surgery. But that's Al.

She asked, "What did Mike looked like?"

"He was wearing green scrubs."

That was not the only time that day that Al had us all in stitches. It felt so good to laugh!

# 36

# My Mind Short-Circuits

The next days were full of trips to the hospital downtown, but each saw Al stronger. At first, of course, he could hardly even talk or smile, but within a few days when we came to visit him he said, "Want to come for a walk with me?" So we joined him in shuffling laps around the seventh floor.

Al had a really impressive black eye as the fluids drained down into his face. Since Alden had had an accidental run-in with someone's knee at camp, resulting in a black eye, they were a matched set.

One day when we visited, Eowyn was cold, so she climbed into the hospital bed with Al and the two of them kept each other warm.

Al told us with an enormous grin, "Last night my pen started rolling off the table, and I caught it in midair!" He was *so* incredibly pleased and encouraged to see that his reflexes were still that good.

"Anything you want us to bring you from home?" I asked later as we were leaving.

A grin. Then, "A cheesesteak?"

The staples in Al's head looked like Frankenstein, but he was in good spirits.

Notwithstanding, he was incredibly glad to get back home. The only request he had voiced the whole year was, "If possible, I'd rather not spend any more time in hospitals than necessary." So it was sad when two days later he developed another blood clot and ended up in the local emergency room. He was then transferred by ambulance back to the hospital downtown where the surgeon could monitor him. However, even in the ER, God was with us. We discovered that the father of one of Rebeckah's high school friends was two beds down, so we had a nice visit with him and his wife, and other friends came by to pray with us and then went to help our kids.

A couple days later, Al was released and was grateful to come back home to stay.

This period was the third "overload weekend" for me—the third time I felt stretched beyond my resources. I could hardly think straight. Making decisions was impossible. I was literally incapable of weighing factors even for a simple question like whether one of the kids could have a friend sleep overnight at the last minute. It was weird. I wasn't upset; I just couldn't think. Thankfully, we were surrounded by wonderful friends who carried us through. The church kept sending us meals, and most of all, they kept loving and watching out for our kids. They helped us when we couldn't function on our own.

# 37

## What Do You Do with Anger?

During that period, Eowyn wrote a post in which she asked people not to be angry with God on our behalf.

Anger is a common and normal part of grief. When experts describe the "stages" of grieving, they include anger among them.

Anger can't be all bad because the Psalms are full of expressions of the psalmists' anger, and throughout the Bible God himself is described as being angry. Some things are *right* to be angry about: injustice, oppression, cruelty, child abuse, sex trafficking. God himself hates those things! Even things like sickness and death were not part of God's original creation; they came about when Adam and Eve sinned and broke God's perfect world (Genesis 3). Death is an affront to him.

The important thing about anger—or anything else—is *what we do with it*. The psalmists did not simply "vent" at God and then walk away, and I am not advocating that. Their honesty was part of a process of trying to grapple with God and hold onto faith. Like them, we can bring our anger to God (even if *he* is the one we're upset with!) and wrestle honestly with him, expressing our frustrations, doubts, confusion, or struggles. We can ask him to help us understand, and we can ask him to help us trust him even if we don't understand. I think the Psalms are ample evidence that God wants us to be honest with him, and that when we come *to* God and bring our anger honestly before him, even very vocally, and ask him to help us process it, it is an expression of faith that actually helps move us toward him.

I once had a friend who was mistreated. What was worse was that the person mistreating my friend was a Christian who should have known better. It made me really angry. I had to keep bringing my anger back to the Lord every day, often many times a day. I asked the Lord why he let this happen. I asked him if I should get involved and try to intervene somehow. I prayed for things to turn around. The Lord says "Vengeance is mine. I will repay" (Romans 12:19), so I needed to trust the situation into his hands and ask him to bring his own justice to bear. I prayed to recognize the sinful impulses of my own heart that were as worthy of judgment as whatever was driving the perpetrator's actions. I constantly had to turn it over to the Lord and let go of my anger. The process of doing so kept driving me back to him. I think that was faith.

Alternatively, we can turn our backs on God in anger. We can believe that we know better than he does and that his willingness to let suffering occur is stupid or wrong, or that he doesn't care, or that he is cruel and withholding good from us. Of course, that lie is as old as the Garden of Eden, where Satan fed it to Eve (Genesis 3:4–6). We can withdraw from God and give him the cold shoulder, or let anger and resentment smolder, unexpressed. If we let our hearts live there and become bitter, faith will eventually wither, and we will have allowed anger to move us away from God. When Eowyn asked people not to be angry at God on our behalf, I think she had in mind this second kind of anger.

I will speak only for myself when I say that I can't remember being angry at God about Al's cancer. I don't know why that was. *Maybe* part of it was that Al and I both grew up in homes where our parents loved us unfailingly, and we *knew* it because they constantly showed it in word and deed. When we each came into a relationship with God as our heavenly Father, it was not a stretch to believe that he was that kind of parent too. I think that was our default assumption because of our experience with our own parents. They always wanted what was best for us, even if that was not always what we as kids would have chosen in a particular instance. So maybe our default setting was to believe that, likewise, what God brought into our lives he intended for good.

In any case, others may well have been angry at God about Al's cancer, and if so, I hope they were able to bring their anger directly to God.

# 38

# G-r-a-d-u-a-l Makeover

I may not have been angry at God that Al had cancer, but I definitely had a lousy attitude about one of the ways his health impacted me. Get ready to hear some whining.

I like to bake, but I never learned to like cooking, even after three decades. Menu planning was the worst part of it. As Al struggled with fibromyalgia year after year, he tried one diet after another in the hope of finding something that would help him feel better, and each one created new demands on me as the cook. The only diet that ever made him feel measurably better was eating only fresh fruits and vegetables. I liked that because it meant minimal meal preparation. But the kids were not excited about dinner being simply a big fruit salad. When Rebeckah's Bible study leader at church heard that she had had only fruit salad for dinner, she brought Rebeckah a pork chop because she felt so sorry for her! None of Al's healthy diets sat well with the kids, so I entered the kitchen each day not liking to cook in the first place and knowing that however long I spent working on dinner, either it wouldn't be good for Al or the kids weren't going to want to eat it. It was very discouraging. For a while I prepared double meals each night, which was no fun either.

In August of 2006, Al and I met for four hours with a cancer nutritionist who recommended a new diet that was going to be more demanding than ever. It entailed completely restocking the kitchen from an expensive health food store and then required me to learn a whole new way of cooking. *Again.*

I didn't believe that the new diet was likely to make any difference, and that probably ended up being true. However, I should still have been grateful for Al's sake that we had an idea that might . . . maybe . . . possibly help him feel better. Instead, I was thinking only of the impact this would have on my time and mental resources, and I was *not* excited about it.

Eowyn and Alden, seeing my discouragement and bad humor, took a huge piece of paper, drew various exotic healthy foods on it, taped it up on a wall, handed me a child's toy gun, and said, "Go ahead, Mom. Take it out on the fruits and veggies." I'm not necessarily recommending that as a godly way to deal with a selfish heart, but I definitely appreciated their sensitivity, and the laughter we shared did make me feel better.

As Al had said, having terminal cancer (or in my case, living with a loved one who does) doesn't exempt you from the Lord working on your heart. I remember another day—the morning after Lisa's wedding in May—when I was so upset with Al that I couldn't even sing during worship. Our kids were hurting with the news that the cancer had almost certainly spread to Al's brain, and they wanted to talk to their friends and youth group leaders about it. Al didn't want them to do that until he'd had a chance to tell one of his friends, so that the friend wouldn't hear about it secondhand. I could not believe that Al was willing to gag our kids and deny them the support of the body for the sake of his friend's feelings. I objected, he didn't change his mind, and *I was furious!* I was so steamed I had to leave the service, and when Al saw that, he said, "Hang on. I'm coming with you." We left the service together and talked things through. He relented, we found the kids and told them to go ahead and talk with anyone they needed to, and then Al managed to contact the friend and tell him about the brain swelling.

Theologians talk about "justification" and "sanctification." Justification is about Jesus paying the price for our sins by his death on the cross: the innocent voluntarily dying in place of the guilty. Sanctification is about the Holy Spirit gradually transforming us to be more like Jesus. Unlike the makeover shows on TV, however, this process takes a lifetime and will not be finished until we get to heaven. Fortunately, the Holy Spirit is both incredibly patient and fully committed to the ultimate transformation, because the change is often v-e-r-y slow. He used Al's cancer journey, like everything else through a lifetime, to grow me, one infinitesimal step at a time—tenderly, gently, persistently. I was thankful for that and, being so very far from being like Jesus, I was (and am) *so* grateful for the complete forgiveness that Jesus bought on the cross!

# Fall '06

# 39

## Puddle Prints

In September we had an appointment with the neurosurgeon and the waiting room was packed. Appointments were running a good two hours behind schedule, and frustrated patients were making it known that they weren't happy. I was a little annoyed myself. But, true to form, Al, rather than getting angry and short-tempered, went out of his way to chat with the nurses about what a strenuous day it must be for them and to tell them he appreciated their patience.

The neurosurgeon's care and compassion were outstanding. Yet we thought we sensed behind his professional and sensitive comments that he didn't expect to see Al at his next scheduled appointment, which was three months away. Perhaps we misread him. In any case, he said some wonderful things about Al, including that he had been struck by how magnanimous he was. He said simply and honestly, "You are the kind of person I would like to be when I grow older." It was a rare moment of honest personal connection, and we were touched by his candor and sincerity.

Throughout the process of Al's cancer, I watched person after person notice that there was something unusual about Al. He was genuinely interested in people, and he appreciated whatever large or small thing they did for him and made sure to tell them so. He put himself in their shoes to see things from their perspective, and he went out of his way to encourage them. He always had time for people, not as some kind of duty, but because he loved them.

As just one example, after Al's brain surgery, he knew the names of all the nurses and aides (and at least one of the janitors), how and why they got into nursing, what their career hopes were, and other things of importance about them.

Al once wrote about Psalm 84:6, which talks about the pilgrim on the way to Zion, making the Valley of Baca into a place of springs. He said he wished he were an illustrator because he pictured it as some-one traveling through a desert and leaving puddles as footprints. He thought it would make a good kids' cartoon. He was a lot like that pil-grim, leaving puddles of grace and graciousness in people's lives every-where he went.

I know that Al's delight in people was because the Lord was in him. The character of God worked into Al's heart was noticeable and attractive. It was a living-out of the verse I learned as a kid, "Let your light so shine before men, that they may see your good works, and glo-rify your Father which is in heaven" (Matthew 5:16 KJV).

Al was not perfect. Thinking back on our early years together, he was sometimes a knucklehead. But through all the years I knew him, he was growing in a Godward direction. He was quick to listen and to change, quick to look for his own fault in a situation and apologize, slow to accuse or find fault in others, and quick to forgive. He was courageous to speak up for people who couldn't defend themselves. He was becom-ing like Jesus. Not a marshmallowy Hollywood Jesus with a dreamy gaze and his head in the clouds. The real Jesus, who gave up heaven to come down and live in this broken world as a man—a working man, a refugee, a homeless person—and to show us what was really on his Father's heart, with the divine grit to love sacrificially and to be what human beings were created to be. That's what Al was growing toward.

It was a blessing to know him, and an even greater blessing to be his wife.

# 40

## Wasting Away

After Al's brain surgery in late August, a gradual medical decline followed through the fall and early winter.

Al developed blood clots in both legs, which proved to be more painful and life-impacting than the cancer itself. For a time they were so bad that he couldn't walk. He was again reduced to crawling from the couch to the bathroom. We set up a bedroom for him in the room off the kitchen so that he didn't have to go up and down stairs. He could not exercise, which affected his general health and spirits. But blood thinners and compression stockings slowly helped. Then he had whole brain radiation for several weeks, which left him fatigued and unstable. (It also left him bald, and Alasdair shaved his own head in solidarity.) He coughed up small amounts of blood throughout each day because of the tumors in his lungs. His head ached from the brain swelling, and he had neurological episodes of odd geometric shapes of purple and silver in his left peripheral vision from the brain tumor. But worst of all was his uncomfortable stomach. Eating anything bothered it, so sometimes, especially if he needed to think clearly or speak, teach, write or meet with someone, he would fast most of the day in order to feel a bit better.

There was a lot of sickness in the family that fall too. With each of Al's new symptoms we wondered whether he was catching something, or whether this was the start of a downward trajectory. Sometimes he would have a few bad days and then bounce back and feel a bit better for a while, which was always a welcome reprieve.

We were back in a period of uncertainty, not about the eventual outcome, but about the timing. Scans in November showed that the lung tumors were growing; one was the size of an orange. If we had been in the situation of so many cancer patients, desperately hoping for a cure, such news would have been devastating. But since we knew from the beginning that Al's cancer was terminal, the report was simply a measuring stick that gave us an idea of how the disease was progressing. We expected the November scan would also show spread to the liver, based on how poorly Al was feeling. But the liver was clear at that point, which was a nice surprise.

I remember one night that fall when Alden was sick with vomiting and a high fever. Al felt mildly rotten, and I had nasty seasonal allergies. Eowyn was at church, helping to paint the senior high room, but the three of us sat around the coffee table (where we ate dinner in those days, since it was most comfortable for Al to be on the couch) nibbling wearily at whatever food suited our digestive fortitude. Every now and then one of us would observe, "We're a lively crew, aren't we?"

And yet there was something cozy about being in a warm house on a cool evening, waiting for the rain that was forecast to start during the night and watching people drive by in the dark on their way home from work. I thought of homeless people in the city, who must have felt differently about the coming rain. And of families who would not want to sit in the same room with each other.

Despite everything, we had an awful lot to be thankful for.

# 41

## Gifts in Grief

The fall was full of special gifts from the Lord. For one, the weather and the colored leaves were the most gorgeous I'd seen in Philadelphia in the twenty-seven years we had lived there. Lots of people commented on what a beautiful fall it was that year. That may not seem like much, but we received it as a tender love note from the Lord, lavishing extravagant beauty on us to feast our eyes and encourage our spirits.

Wobbly as he was, Al was able to go to Westminster's convocation and see colleagues, students, and other friends, which delighted him. He was able to speak in chapel once and to give a few lectures in a class on the prophetic books of the Bible. And he had the privilege of giving the official charge to Doug Green at Doug's inauguration as full professor. What a joy that was.

Doug and Mike, Al's colleagues, came by every week to visit and to mull over Bible passages or particular issues in the field of biblical studies. Al loved those times.

We had wonderful visits with old friends and former students from all over the country and the world, and each visit was a blessing. We went to Vermont to see my parents, whom Al hadn't seen since his diagnosis—since neither he nor they had felt up to traveling. My sister from Maine drove six hours each way to join us there. The husband of my sister in Michigan happened to be in Vermont on business, so he came from across the state to be there too.

In October, the whole Groves clan came to Philadelphia for a get-together to celebrate Al's mom's seventy-fifth birthday. We had a lovely time, and Al got Mom and Dad to tell stories from their childhoods, some of which had us hooting with laughter.

Every one of those things was a precious gift. Most of them we had not anticipated, and the fact that Al was here for them was something we did not take for granted. All of it was God's mercy, and we were thankful.

# 42

# Problem Solved

Numerous times during the year Al was dying I thought about the fact that in any given field, some problems are straightforward and easy to fix, and others are much more complex. For instance, if you have a strep throat, at least here in the First World, the doctor gives you antibiotics, and presto—in twenty-four hours you are usually on your way to feeling better. But if you have high blood pressure and high cholesterol, you're going to have to change your diet, exercise, and be disciplined about it for a lifetime. It's a much more involved and drawn out process.

When I thought about other things people struggle or suffer with, I felt as if Al's cancer fell very much into the easy-fix category. I do acknowledge that my understanding of "fix" may not be standard. For many or most people, fixing cancer means being healed from it, going into permanent remission. But while "permanent" remission means that cancer won't kill you, eventually something else will: the death rate among humans is still one hundred percent.

For me, "fix" has a bigger frame of reference. I have in mind an eternal fix that includes being set free from death forever. In Al's case, it was true that unless God decided to perform a miracle of healing—which we knew he certainly could and which we still prayed for—Al would die. But he would immediately be in heaven with Jesus, with the indescribable joy of seeing the Father face-to-face, free from pain, tears, and death. What could be more wonderful for him? Jesus's death and resurrection are the answer to death, and that answer is simple and straightforward. Al had to do nothing but trust and rest in him.

Many people who deal with cancer and other potentially fatal diseases face the more difficult situation of constant suspense, not knowing if the disease will end their lives or if they will survive. Those ups and downs create their own unique suffering.

Other people have to deal with chronic pain and illness. We knew from Al's years of fibromyalgia how terribly hard that can be: suffering while knowing there is little hope that the suffering will end in this life. Jesus is the answer to that suffering too, but it involves such perseverance of faith that I feel weary just thinking about it.

Still others face the even harder pain of seeing their children or others they love walk away from faith, or make choices and walk down roads that will lead to destruction. Jesus is the answer to their challenges too, but that path is tortuous, protracted, and difficult.

In so many ways, we really had it easy. All we had to do was rest in the Lord, and Al would shortly be with him in heaven. It was as simple and as glorious as that.

# 43

# Resting Place

When Al and I discussed burial, cremation, and related issues, his concern was for those of us who were left behind. He wanted us to make a choice that *we* were comfortable with. I decided that it would be nice to have a grave—a specific location—that the kids and I could visit in the future. So, in October, I went to the cemetery to pick out a gravesite.

Usually people pick out graves way ahead of time or under pressure after an unexpected death. If the former, the grave is something they expect to need someday in the far-off future. If the latter, the choice of a grave is yet one more baffling detail in the midst of the shock and numbness of sudden grief. It was odd for me to be between those two extremes. I was not under pressure to choose a grave in a matter of hours, yet I *was* choosing a gravesite for someone who was going to need it very soon.

Dying is a strenuous physical process. I learned that from watching Al, and then my dad, and then my mom die in successive years. Disposing of a loved one's body is very physical too. I have watched one body be lowered into the earth and another be slid into the heat of a crematorium furnace. Death is very physical, and there is no way around it. Even the sure knowledge of the glory of heaven ahead, while it takes the sting out of the sadness of death, does not mitigate its physicality.

I knew that picking out a gravesite would be a very in-your-face reminder of that fact, and I dreaded it. So I asked the Lord to meet me in the midst of that process and he did.

My friend Nan went with me (bless her!) and it wasn't as painful as I had anticipated. There is a cemetery within walking distance from our house where we had often biked when the kids were little, so it was a no-brainer to choose a spot there. We drove around looking at the different sections and we found ourselves saying things like "This area has a pretty view" and "That's too close to a busy road" and "Those woods across the way won't ever be developed, so that's nice." Hearing ourselves say those things made it almost feel like buying a house, which made us laugh. Somehow we were able to detach the selection process from the sadness that was necessitating it, so we had a nice time together. We enjoyed the serenity of the quiet graveyard and its peaceful beauty.

I have a tendency to make decisions more difficult than they need to be. So when it took me several visits back to the cemetery before I finally decided on a site, I wondered if I was being silly and belaboring the process. But in retrospect, I don't think so. I love the area I chose and I love to go there. It is in a quiet, secluded area right by some woods that remind me a little bit of my childhood home in Vermont, especially in the fall. It is a place of beauty and peace.

We have each visited Al's grave many times, individually and in groups. The more energetic members of the family sometimes run there and back (three miles round trip from our front door). Alasdair and Lauren have taken their girls to "Grandpa Groves's" grave, and Eowyn and I took pictures of her there in her wedding gown. When I go in the spring and the dogwood trees are in blossom or in the fall when the colored leaves are so pretty, I think of the wonders Al is seeing now in the Lord's presence and of the new heavens and new earth ahead that will make this world's most spectacular natural beauty fade to gray.

I am grateful that the Lord met me in the business of choosing Al's grave. He is so tender.

# 44

# Love One Another

As the fall went on, Al started to sound more and more like the apostle John. In John's old age, the vast truth of what God had done in Christ seemed to sort of clarify and boil down to the simple importance of love—God's amazing love for people and the supreme call to love each other. Al seemed to be undergoing that same shift in focus.

He preached on 1 John 3:1–3 in chapel at Westminster in October with that in mind (available at www.wts.edu/resources/media, as of the writing of this book). His consistent drumbeat could be summarized by the following:

> Love each other as God has loved you. Recognize and cherish the grace and forgiveness you have received in Christ, and then live out of that grace in your interactions with others. We cannot control what others do to us, but we are always responsible for how we respond, and that response should be prompted by and should flow out of the costly forgiveness we have received from God. If we don't radically love others, there is a disconnect in our lives that shows that we have not really grasped the love God has lavished on us. As we meditate on and really understand the grace God has shown us, we should be willing to lay down our lives for each other, to walk in the light, to repent of our sins, to ask forgiveness and to forgive each other, to believe the best about each other, to give the benefit of the doubt and to be charitable toward each other.

I felt as if Al could have sat down and written something like 1 John, if John himself hadn't already done so. I guess it's not surprising that there would be something about the approach of death to sharpen one's vision and give a clearer perspective on truth and reality—and on what matters most to the Lord.

# 45

## Love in the Details

Both Alasdair and Alden are passionate Eagles fans. In the fall of 2006, neither of them had ever been to a professional football game, nor had Al. Al had the idea that he would love to take his boys to an Eagles game before he died. (He also took his girls to a live performance of "The Lion King" at the Kimmel Center.) However, when we found out how hard it was to get tickets and how *frightfully* expensive they were, we laid that idea to rest.

But our friend Jim and some other people were not satisfied with that, and through an apparent miracle and the generosity of friends, we ended up with tickets—to the Cowboys game, for controversial former Eagle Terrell Owens's first time back in Philly! I wish you could have seen Alasdair and Alden's faces when Al told them the news.

Of course, we didn't know if Al would be in physical shape to go to a game in October, or if the weather would make it impossible, or how he would be able to keep his leg elevated during the game. But it turned out that he was strong enough to manage it, and the day was sunny, in the 70s. Alasdair and Alden went all out painting up for the game, which was great fun.

The seats our friend Jim got were tremendous, down low on the 30-yard line behind the Eagles bench. And get this: *There was a wall that ran right beside Al's seat where he could put his leg up while he sat!* That detail was something the Lord threw in as an extra reminder of his love and care. He was very much involved in this wonderful day.

Our guys came home almost deaf and mute from cheering, stumbling over each other to report, "It was a barn burner! In the last twelve seconds Lito Sheppard intercepted the ball and ran 102 yards for a touchdown!" All of them were flying high from the excitement. Al was thoroughly exhausted, but it was absolutely worth it.

What a gift it was. That they could go to a game at all, that it was the Dallas game, that T. O. was shut down by the Eagles defense, that Al had the strength to go, that the weather was beautiful, that the crowd was over-the-top electrified, and that it was a down-to-the-wire fantastic game, made it a day none of them will ever, ever forget. It was a gift—from Jim, from friends who had chipped in for tickets, and from the Lord, who oversaw the details right down to the weather and a wall for a footrest.

For our guys it was more than just a football game. It was a chance to enjoy a special experience together, to build a memory that the boys will cherish in the years ahead, and to see the Lord's generous, tender love. The Lord may not care about who wins a football game, but he does love his children and he delights to pour out that love in personalized, intimate, generous, overflowing ways. He does it all the time, for all of us. But I often don't notice. I go around living as if things "just happen" or "just work out," rather than realizing that they come to me directly from God's loving hand. He was so clearly involved in the details of the whole day, but it wasn't until he provided that wall for Al's feet that I saw it myself. It seems that, unless God writes with fireworks, I don't read his messages.

# 46

# He Lived Them Both—For Us

As I mentioned, Al continued to read through the Psalms once a month during the year he was dying, as he had done for many, many years. It refreshed his soul. On one of his read-throughs, he noticed something he had not seen before about Psalms 22 and 23 in relation to each other. That is one of the beauties of Scripture: you can read something hundreds of times and never exhaust its riches. Here is what he observed:

> The number 23 follows the number 22. Basic arithmetic. Any five-year-old knows this as soon as they learn to count. Apparently I had forgotten how to count when I read the Psalms. Psalms 22 and 23 are next-door neighbors; they follow numerically. And they follow one another as the Spirit intended when he led those who organized the Psalter in their ordering of the Psalms. But somehow I never saw the connection. In fact, I have been reading and rereading each of these psalms recently, treating them as if they had nothing to do with one another, silos standing beside one another, containing two different, unrelated kinds of spiritual nourishment.
>
> David is the human author of both, but no occasion in his life is provided for either psalm. Placed together, they tell a story of the soul. One poem begins with David in the depths of despair, crying out to God; the following one begins with what is perhaps the most well-known picture of peace in all of literature. God far off becomes God near and caring. A soul in despair becomes a soul at peace. The two psalms could hardly begin more differently.

Psalm 22:1: "My God, my God, why have you forsaken me? Why are you so far from saving me, from the words of my groaning?"

Psalm 23:1: "The LORD is my shepherd; I shall not want."

An abandoning God becomes a God who is a shepherd who takes care of his sheep so well that the sheep have no need. Taken together, as they should be, these psalms give us spiritual whiplash, ricocheting us from a God who is somehow distant to a God who is near.

Jesus, the son of David, used the opening lines of Psalm 22 on the cross. There may be no more significant cry of anguish in the history of the universe: The Son of God, eternally in fellowship with his Father, cried out to him in agony at what appeared to be God abandoning him. Why? We know the answer, even if we do not fully understand it: Jesus became sin, he took upon himself God's wrath, he took the punishment we deserved, and in that moment God the Father turned his back on his Son and the Son died, not at the hands of men, but at the hand of God punishing sin (our sin, not his). Because he carried my sin, Jesus, separated from his Father, cried out: "My God, my God, why have you forsaken me?"

But the Father did not leave his Son in the grave. The Father, the Shepherd, rescued his Son, the sheep, and brought him safely out of the valley of the shadow of death, alive. He raised Jesus from the dead and exalted him to his throne in heaven. Jesus experienced to the very fullest both the agony and abandonment of Psalm 22 and the peace and security of Psalm 23. He lived them both in the most extreme way.

And now, Jesus has become the Good Shepherd. The forsaken one becomes the caring shepherd, leading those who hear his voice into permanent pastures of peace. What incredible love! The One who was abandoned because of what we did does not abandon us. He walked through death's valley alone, for our sake, but now he does not leave us to walk there alone.

I am now walking through the valley of the shadow of death. But I walk through it hand-in-hand with the One who walked there and emerged alive on the other end. His rod and staff, his CROSS, they comfort me. I know that he will not only walk with me but will bring me safely into life on the other side of the valley, and therefore I'm not afraid.

Psalm 22? Because Jesus experienced the agony of that psalm on the cross for my sake, as I am in Christ, I will never have to sing it. In fact, I cannot sing it. Because, through his Son's death, God has not abandoned me and never will.

Psalm 23? Because the Father, the Shepherd, delivered Jesus from the power of death, as I am in Christ, I can and do sing that psalm. The Lord is indeed my Shepherd, and Jesus the Good Shepherd cares for me in every possible way, every day of my life, and through the valley of death.

He even sets a feast for us before our true enemies—sin and death (the residents of the valley), whom he has defeated. None are worthy of the banquet—that's what grace is all about—but he grants it to us out of his great love and compassion as we believe.

# 47

# More Alive than Ever

Two men in our church died during the fall of 2006. Al wrote the following in November:

> We had a memorial service for a dear friend from church today. I was struck during the reading of the Scripture (2 Corinthians 4:7–18) by the words that God's power is shown even in our dying bodies. I can honestly say that in these past few months I have felt more alive than almost any other period in my life. God has been near and showing his goodness at every turn, large issues and small. While I would not have chosen it this way, the recent months have been a special time of knowing and seeing God and his love in powerful ways.
>
> While the perishable flesh is clearly fading for me, life only grows more vivid. We await only the putting on of the imperishable body, which means putting off the perishable. The resurrection. The great hope we have in Christ. May God give us all a fresh vision of that hope, and may he loose the power of the resurrection in our lives as we live from day to day.
>
> Death, the perishing of this body, is not the end, but a gateway to life in his presence, a life which is beyond what we can currently imagine, a life where we are face-to-face with Jesus at all times and able to worship him with total freedom. How great is our Savior and his salvation for us!

As Al's health declined, I thought about Psalm 17:15. It says, "As for me, I shall behold your face in righteousness; when I awake, I shall be satisfied with your likeness."

What might it be like to fall asleep in this life and wake up in heaven? Of course we don't know much about what heaven will be like, except that God will be there and it will be more wonderful than we can possibly imagine. Much of what we tend to picture about heaven is actually part of the final resurrection when we will receive our resurrected bodies. But sometimes if I daydream about waking up in heaven, something like the following image drifts into my mind and makes me smile:

I picture a cozy, rustic, clean, and bright one-room log cabin perched high on the side of a mountain akin to the Alps. The walls and floors of the cabin are rough-hewn boards. There is a table covered with a red and white checked cloth; bright red and pink geraniums are blooming riotously along the windowsill; bright, warm, morning sunshine is streaming in through the open windows, and clear, clean, cool, mountain air drifts in with it. In my daydream I wake up in a cozy bed piled with down comforters, aware of the surroundings in a general sort of way. But my attention is on Jesus, who sits next to the bed, smiling down at me with the most wonderful eyes and welcoming me home. "When I wake, I shall be satisfied with your likeness."

What glory! No need for caffeine that morning.

# WINTER '06–'07

# 48

## Struggling to Share

In December, I wrote the following post:

> Another thing that has been challenging has been seeing things in
> my own heart that need to change. I see once again that in many
> ways I don't have a clue about how to love: how to love God, how
> to love people, or how to love the amazing and wonderful man
> whom God gave me to be my husband. Being an independent New
> Englander, and not natively inclined to vulnerability, or to sharing
> my heart readily, or to intimacy, I am so bad at nurturing relation-
> ships of any kind. The Holy Spirit has made some progress in me in
> that area over the past two years, but I think I'm still barely taking
> baby steps. "They say" that just before you die your life passes
> before your eyes. A couple of weeks ago I felt as if the years of our
> marriage were passing in review before my eyes, and I saw how
> much more deeply I could have shared my heart, my life, myself
> with Al in these twenty-eight years. There is so much I want to say
> to him even now, but I struggle to, even though I know I will wrestle
> with regret for a lifetime if I don't. I'd be grateful if you'd pray for me
> about that. I also see how selfish, self-oriented, and self-absorbed
> I am.

Thankfully, Al and I did have the conversation I'd asked people to
pray for.

One night I took a deep breath and said, "There are so many ways I
haven't loved you well, and I'm sorry. I know I am really bad at relaxing
and that I'm too busy and work all the time, and that's not good for our

relationship. I focus on the kids and neglect you. I don't communicate well. I don't share my inner thoughts unless pushed. I don't like to open my heart and be vulnerable."

"You're too hard on yourself."

"No, it's true. I know I've sometimes let resentment build and that when circumstances have contributed to that, I've let it happen. Sometimes I've brought that part of my heart to the Lord for surgery and healing, but sometimes I haven't. All along I should have been talking to you about it, but I didn't want to. I'm sorry. I love you, and I'm so sorry."

His response? "I've always felt very loved by you. When I think of what I am thankful for, after the Lord, you are what I cherish more than anything or anyone. You have loved me so well, and I have always been thankful for you and in love with you."

What a husband.

I know my own sin, and I will always know that I could and should have loved Al better in so many ways. But I'm thankful for the Lord's forgiveness, and I'm glad I had a chance to talk to Al about it.

# 49

## Last Gifts

On December 17, Al turned fifty-four. The previous January, when we had first learned that there was something in his lungs, and then in February when it was confirmed to be melanoma, we didn't know if he would still be with us in December. I had trouble believing he would be. But he was. His health had become tenuous, but he was still here.

We cherished each day Al was with us. Of course we should be doing that all the time, with all of our loved ones, since any of us could die at any time. We should be living as if each day were our last—and also as if it were the last day for the people we love, telling them we love them and saying all the things we would regret not having said. We knew Al's departure was coming soon, so we appreciated each day the Lord gave us together.

It's odd to buy gifts for someone who is going to leave this world soon. We gave Al warm, comfy slippers, favorite snacks, and a warm throw blanket made of fabric we knew he would enjoy. Alasdair and Lauren printed up a book of photos of family Christmases through the years, and Al took it to bed with him every night to savor the pictures, the memories, and the precious relationships he had with each of us.

Two days before his birthday, at the Westminster staff Christmas luncheon, it was announced that the faculty had decided to rename the Westminster Hebrew Institute for Al. He had founded the center in the 1980s to harness the power and capabilities of computing to enhance the study of the Hebrew Bible, and the center helped produce the databases that underlie many of the Bible software products available today.

In December 2006, the institute became The J. Alan Groves Center for
Advanced Biblical Research. Al was extremely honored by the gesture,
and perhaps even more touched by the friendship and thoughtfulness
it evidenced.

We didn't know how much longer Al would be with us, but it was
an unexpected blessing to celebrate his birthday and Christmas with
him one last time.

# 50

## Unanticipated Goodness

On January 16, 2007, Al wrote the following:

A year ago on January 16, 2006, Martin Luther King Day, we learned that I had a year or so to live. We have grieved, but always with hope in the resurrection we have through faith in Christ. While we would not have chosen it this way, we have seen God's goodness, nearness, steadfast love, and faithfulness in unprecedented fashion. We have rested in the reality that he is absolutely in control and he is good.

We have seen the goodness of the Lord through so many of you. We have been overwhelmed by the outpouring of kindness.

God has continued to be a father to me. He still ferrets out the issues in my heart and leads me in repentance. The need for sanctification never ends; difficult circumstances have not given me a free pass. My failure to respond well to people or to reach out to others has been particularly an area in which I have been challenged. As painful as this kind of "heart surgery" can be, I am reminded each time he puts his finger on something that he is there and is ever loving me. It may seem strange to some, but he shows his fatherly love and concern by continuing to love me through discipline (Hebrews 12:5–6).

We have peace and hope afresh in the resurrection, and we are learning about grieving with hope.

Walking through the valley of the shadow of death, we are not alone. We walk with One who has walked it already and has emerged alive on the other end, who leads us through that valley, and who will lead to life all who trust him. We have had wonderful care, which we see as part of God's providential hand in sustaining us. God alone heals. He does so in many ways. Sometimes his purposes are best served as we put off the perishable and put on the imperishable. The Lord gives, and the Lord takes away. Blessed be his name.

# 51

## New Limitations

On January 18, Al fell. It was because he tried to run a short distance and apparently his equilibrium and coordination, which were okay for walking, weren't up to running. He hit hard, scraping his chin, hands, and knees, but he took the brunt of the fall on his abdomen. In fact he landed so hard that at first he wondered if he had broken a rib, though that turned out not to be the case.

The complicating factor was that he was crossing a busy street when he fell. The fall was so sudden and the impact so forceful that he ended up sprawled in the middle of the street, stunned. Thankfully, there was a big enough gap in the traffic that oncoming cars had plenty of time to slow down and stop before they reached him.

He told us, "I couldn't get up, even to my hands and knees, but once I could breathe, I slowly army-crawled to the far curb."

The first car in the line of traffic happened to be driven by one of our neighbors, who stopped and helped Al get to his feet. He had been walking to meet someone for breakfast at a diner two blocks from our house. (I had offered to drive him but he was determined to walk.) In true Al fashion, once he regained his breath, his balance, and his composure, he cautiously walked the remaining block to the restaurant and had breakfast. But after that fall he never felt the same again physically.

Although we knew from the start that Al's cancer was terminal and were thus spared the roller coaster of wondering whether he would survive or not, we still lived with the uncertainty of timing. Throughout the fall season, each time he felt poorly we wondered if it was a permanent downturn or just a passing virus. Many times he felt unwell but then improved. His symptoms were constantly up and down, with a gradual, overall, downward trend.

Before he fell, Al had been feeling sort of lousy, and we had been taking a wait-and-see attitude to determine if that was a temporary thing, or the result of decreasing the steroids, or if it represented a progression of the cancer and a more permanent downturn in his health. After he fell, his health took a marked decline. He felt very ill and a bit shaken up, and in the days that followed, he was increasingly uncomfortable in his abdomen, top to bottom and front to back. Looking back on it later, it was clear that sometime between the November scans and the January tumble, the cancer had spread to his liver. The impact of his fall just exacerbated what was already going on inside him. But at the time, we didn't know that. It was clear that he was declining, but the timeline was still unknown.

The Lord sometimes calls us to walk uncertain paths with only his presence being completely clear. On the path he chose for us, we discovered that his presence was enough.

# 52

# Facing Death
# with Our Eyes Wide Open

As Al declined in January, I was struck by Psalm 89:48. It says, "What man can live and never see death? Who can deliver his soul from the power of Sheol?" Death is a part of what happens to people in this world. It is not "natural" because it was not part of God's original creation; it came into the world as a result of our sin. But it is "natural" in that it eventually happens to every single person.

Yet in our society we tend to try to keep it at arm's length. We shield ourselves and our children as much as possible from any contact with death. Lots of people manage to reach adulthood without ever having been to a funeral. I can understand this. If this life is all there is and you don't know what (if anything) comes after it, death is scary. Who wants to expose their children unnecessarily to that frightening eventuality? It is easier to live in denial of the possibility of death and to pretend that it can be put off or ignored, if not actually avoided.

However, in other times and in other parts of the world, such a stance is not practicable. A child in Africa who has lost both of her parents to AIDS comes face-to-face with mortality all the time. For her, death is a cold, hard reality of everyday life. She knows the answer to the question, "What man can live and never see death?" No one.

I have often thought that people who live with a constant awareness that they and their loved ones could easily die tomorrow have an advantage over us. As I read the thoughts of the Pilgrims and other people of faith who lived with that awareness, I see that it put their earthly lives in perspective. It set them in the context of eternity in a way that was helpful and healthy and that affected their priorities.

The second question of Psalm 89:48—"Who can deliver his soul from the power of Sheol?"—was probably simply another way of stating the first question, just in slightly stronger terms. That is common in Hebrew poetry. The answer to both questions is simple: No one can escape death.

But since Jesus came, there is a different and surprising answer to the second question. For those who trust in Jesus's resurrection triumph over death and in his promise that his followers will also live after death—with him in a place beyond our most fantastic imaginations—there actually *is* Someone who can deliver their souls from the power of Sheol. That is radical and mold-shattering.

Because of that, we have always encouraged our kids to come along with us to funerals of people who belonged to Jesus. In the midst of the deep and real grief, there is also such joy. For me, that's where the rubber of Christianity really hits the road.

Partway through the year that Al was dying, one of our kids commented that death had taken seven or eight of our family's friends in the preceding year and a half, which had been hard. And yet it helped us realize that none of us is immune to death; we will each face it when the appointed time comes for us. Realizing that, rather than running from it, made the promise of heaven concrete, precious, and important in the here and now—even for teenagers.

# 53

# What a Difference a Week Makes

By January 23, Al was feeling distinctly less well than he had a week earlier. He was experiencing extreme fatigue, significantly compromised coordination and balance, and a great deal of abdominal pain.

It's remarkable, really, what a difference one week can make. Every Tuesday Al went to the local hospital for a routine blood test to monitor his blood thinners. For most of the fall, when he was weak from radiation, I drove him there, but for several weeks leading up to mid-January he drove himself. On Tuesday, January 16, he drove, dropping Alden off at school on the way, parking a couple of blocks from the hospital, walking in, getting the test, walking back to the car, and then driving home. In contrast, on January 23 I drove him to the front door and procured a wheelchair to wheel him the hundred yards or so to the blood drawing station. It was a major undertaking for Al to slowly walk twenty or thirty feet from the car to the wheelchair. After we got home from the test, he slept for three hours. We thought some of that might be because his steroid dosage needed to be increased slightly, but we were not counting on it.

It was pretty clear that we were heading into the end stages of the journey. Our friend Michael, who is an oncology nurse, came over and talked to us about what to expect in those last stages. That was hard and sobering but very helpful. Al and I talked a bit about logistics, but not a lot about death itself at that point. I think partly he was just too tired.

As I thought about the symptoms Al would experience and the fact that the end really was upon us—that Al really was going to leave us—I had trouble wrapping my mind around it. It reminded me of the onset of labor—something you know is coming, but that still takes you a little bit by surprise when it actually starts.

The labor of dying was about to begin.

# 54

# A Changing Prayer

During the following week, Al became extremely uncomfortable. The cancer in his liver, aggravated by his hard fall, was causing him abdominal pain. Visual episodes caused by one of the brain tumors increased. Some of his cognitive functions were becoming affected. He had trouble finding words and had to back up and start sentences over again to get them to come out right, and sometimes his speech was a bit slurred. The thoughts were okay in his head; they just didn't come out smoothly.

He could no longer type, partly because of compromised brain function and partly because he couldn't always feel his fingers, so he couldn't reply to emails. That was terribly hard on him. Communicating with people was incredibly important to him, and it caused him grief to fail to respond to people. He agonized over email responses that he would not be able to write. During his physical decline, I think that might have been the piece that was hardest for him to relinquish. I typed up and sent out a last few emails from him and put a notice on his email account explaining why he could no longer reply to people, and that eased his mind somewhat. In some ways his exhaustion also softened the hardship.

On Monday, January 29, we started hospice care. For those who fight cancer with the hope of beating it, starting hospice may feel like defeat. In our case, it was actually something of a relief. In fact, we realized we should have started hospice sooner, as is often the case. Al had become so uncomfortable that the top priority was pain and nausea control, and the hope of it was like water on dry ground. On Monday night a nurse came by and got Al registered. The hospice nurses were committed to making him more comfortable, and they were wonderful. I can't say enough about how tremendous all of our medical professionals were from start to finish!

On Wednesday, January 31, a nurse came again. We asked her, "From your experience, how much time would you estimate we have?"

"Maybe five to six weeks."

Al was so weak and uncomfortable by then that after she left he said, with a little anguish, "I don't think I can do this for five or six weeks." He was brave, but he was worn out. For months we had been asking the Lord to lengthen Al's time here, but now we started asking people to pray that the time would be short.

That night Al felt miserable. But the next day we got some anti-nausea medication that worked better. As it took effect, I could see his body relax. What a blessing! My friend Sheri had been coming over on Thursdays to help with whatever needed to be done, and when she came, she helped me strategize and organize for this next phase. Together we helped Al move upstairs, since the smell of food in the kitchen made him more nauseous. None of the three of us realized how weak he had become in the preceding twenty-four hours. It took forty-five minutes for Al, Sheri, and me to get him upstairs, and I actually was not sure he was going to make it.

The following night neither Al nor I got much sleep. He was disoriented and stumbling around, and I worried that he might lurch toward the stairs and fall down them.

On Friday, February 2, the hospice team said that he should not walk at all and ordered a hospital bed set up for us, which was great. The only bad thing was that Al had to sit in a rocking chair for an hour and a half while it was assembled. He was so weak, and it took so much out of him that I genuinely was not sure if he was going to survive or if I should tell all the kids to come immediately from work and school to say their goodbyes. Once he eased gratefully into that bed, he never got out of it.

Whereas on Wednesday the nurse had said "five to six weeks," on Friday she revised her estimate to "Well, not less than a week." And two days later she guessed it would be that day or the next. The Lord was answering our prayers that the time would be short.

# 55

## Saying Good-Bye

That evening and the next morning we had such sweet, poignant, wonderful times with Al. We talked about the blessings we had shared over our respective lifetimes together and were able to tell Al how much we loved him, to thank him for the ways he had blessed us, and to say intentional goodbyes. Al likewise expressed his love and thankfulness for each of us. We assured him, "We all release you. You are free to go. When Jesus comes and calls you, jump up and run to him and don't look back or worry about us; we will be cheering you on from this side." We meant it.

Other friends came by, and we called Al's parents and other family members so that he could tell them goodbye too. It was such a gift to have the opportunity to do that. We knew that there was no cure for Al's cancer and that, barring a miracle, he would die from it, so we had the freedom to accept that and to prepare to let him go. Sometimes, in situations where there has been hope for a cure, even once the end is obvious, people are not able or willing to accept it. They don't want to talk about the reality that the person is about to die so they miss the chance to say goodbye and thank you.

Friday night, Alasdair and I split the job of keeping watch over Al. By the morning we were both completely exhausted and knew we could not do another night like that. Two friends from church started making phone calls, and they came up with a list of men who would be willing to come for half a night to sit with Al. They were working men with jobs and families, but they were willing to give up most of a night's sleep to love Al and to help us. In the end, we only needed that help for one night, but it was humbling to receive such love.

Saturday afternoon some close friends came over to say goodbye, and that weekend, Alasdair and Lauren had a large crowd of college friends staying with them who came over and visited us and sang around Al's bed. He loved it. That night, the first two men on the night shift volunteer list cared for Al while the rest of us got some sleep.

# 56

# Free at Last

Sunday morning, February 4, while the family went to church, I sat with Al. We had always loved to read aloud to each other throughout our twenty-eight years of marriage, and at that time we were reading *At Home in Mitford* by Jan Karon. Al dozed off and on, and I alternated between reading to him when he was awake and writing his obituary when he slept. It was a bit surreal.

As the day went on, death began to gain the upper hand in Al's body. It was hard to see him suffer. He was terribly thirsty, and we were only partially able to quench his thirst because it was hard for him to swallow. More than a drop or two of water at a time tended to make him choke. For me, that was one of the hardest things in the whole process. He could speak only with difficulty, and we couldn't always tell what he wanted or needed. The hospice nurse came by and said she thought he might pass away that day or the next. Therefore, we decided to do the night shift as a family, in pairs, in two-hour shifts. But in the end we all just stayed in his room through the night, packed in like sardines, dozing on any available surface. It was so hard to see Al in such discomfort that I think we were relieved when around 2 a.m. he passed beyond consciously feeling thirst or pain.

At about 10 a.m. Monday, February 5, Al began to struggle to breathe. I had had the impression from books or movies that when that characteristic breathing (what is sometimes called the "death rattle") began, it would be just a handful of minutes before the person passed away. But Al went on and on through the day and into the evening.

We kept talking to him, singing, reading Scripture, praying, touching him, and visiting around his bedside, occasionally laughing—even uproariously on two occasions. He was there in the midst of us, very much a part of us, even when he was to all appearances unresponsive. They say that people in that state can hear what is being said, so we kept including him in our conversations. We kept telling him how much we loved him and were thankful for him, and we kept telling him how thankful (and even envious) we were that he would soon be seeing Jesus face-to-face. Sometimes we laughed, sometimes we cried, and often we sang songs of worship.

Really, it felt like waiting at the airport with someone who is about to take off on an exciting trip. We repeatedly sang "On Jordan's Stormy Banks" and longed, with Al, for him to be on the other side. I kept envisioning standing in semi-darkness on the bank of a river nearly obscured by fog. We could sense the other shore off there through the fog and could even tell that on that far side it was bright daylight. Occasionally the fog would seem to thin enough that the light would brighten up our side of the river a bit. Sometimes you could almost imagine a breeze had wafted a bit of the delicious, pure, clean, sweet air of the other bank across the river and into the room where we all waited amidst the unpleasant smell of death. Sometimes the other shore seemed very, very close. The fog would thin, but never *quite* enough to see the other side clearly. We waited, and waited, and waited. Al was bound for the Promised Land, as the song says, and we were waiting to see him off. Waiting for the Lord to appear out of the mist and take him into the boat and across to the other side. Across to the eternal day, where "no chilling wind, nor poisonous breath" could reach, where "sickness, sighing, pain and death" would be "felt and feared no more." Waiting in the hushed darkness for the light.

Our hope from the beginning was that we could all be there at the moment Al actually died, but after a mostly sleepless Sunday night, we realized that we would need to sleep Monday night. We probably would not all be awake when he died. That was okay because we had had so much wonderful time with him in the preceding days. Each of us let go of that expectation with peace.

Yet the Lord graciously arranged it so that in fact we were all there with him when he died. As it happened, Doug Green was saying to Al, "Soon you will hear the Lord say, 'Well done, good and faithful servant,'" but as he was halfway through his sentence, Al stopped breathing. Doug and Rebeckah called the rest of us, and we bounded up the stairs. Some of us got there only a few seconds before Al's heart stopped beating, but we were all there. After that last breath, his heart simply slowed to a stop, and he was gone.

We all broke out into tears, and smiles, and hugs, and started cheering Al on, shouting, "You're home!"

"Run to Jesus!"

"You're free!"

"You made it!"

"Go get him, Dad!"

"Run!"

We held each other and sobbed through our smiles, just letting the sweet knowledge sink in that Al was set free—from pain, from exhaustion, from labored breathing, from the fibromyalgia that had pummeled him for years and years, from cancer, and from death itself. He was seeing Jesus face-to-face, wrapped in the warm embrace of his Savior. There was no room at that point for sadness. This wasn't something we intellectually decided. It simply couldn't fit in that room or in our hearts at that moment.

The Lord himself finished the sentence that Doug had begun: "Well done, good and faithful servant!"

Then we simply had to sing something. Nothing short of a song would do to express the relief, and joy, and turbulence of emotions swelling up out of our hearts. So we sang with every bit of gusto in our souls the song "On Jordan's Stormy Banks I Stand."

On Jordan's stormy banks I stand,
And cast a wishful eye
To Canaan's fair and happy land,
Where my possessions lie.
O'er all those wide, extended plains
Shines one eternal day;

There God the Son forever reigns,
And scatters night away.

*Refrain:*
I am bound (echo: I am bound), I am bound (echo: I am
bound),
I am bound for the Promised Land.
I am bound (echo: I am bound), I am bound (echo: I am
bound),
I am bound for the Promised Land.

No chilling winds nor poisonous breath
Can reach that healthful shore;
Sickness and sorrow, pain and death,
Are felt and feared no more.

*Refrain*

When shall I reach that happy place,
and be forever blest?
When shall I see my Father's face,
And in His bosom rest?*

*Refrain*

What a celebration it was! We knew that sadness would set in soon enough, but for that night we felt only joy, intense and exhilarating. And relief. I remember walking around heaving sigh after sigh of relief, feeling the tension, concern, and adrenaline drain out of my body.

Thank you, Lord, that death is undone!

---

* The original lyrics, by Samuel Stennett in 1787, have statements rather than questions in the last verse and "Oh, who will come and go with me?" as the third line of the refrain, but this is the way we sing it.

# 57

# A Life Remembered

The next week was a blur of details and decisions. Thankfully, I had been able to make all the biggest decisions ahead of time. I ache for folks who have to deal with all of that in the shock and numbness of a sudden, unexpected death. (Word to the wise: It's never too early to talk about death/funeral/burial details with your loved ones.)

The Lord carried us. He carried us directly, by his Spirit, and he carried us by means of the love of friends and family who supported us.

He carried us as the hope of heaven was so real, and so close, and so tangible, that we basked in its light and warmth. Al was *there* in heaven! Imagining what it was like for Al to see Jesus face-to-face, to experience the glories of heaven with old and new friends, to worship with full abandon—these thoughts filled our minds and hearts and carried us along like a mighty river.

And he carried us through people. Alasdair's wife Lauren was the only one of us who still had her wits about her, and she was incredible. As we tried to choose a date for the memorial service, it slowly dawned on us that we should check the calendar of the church where the service would be held, but Lauren had already done that. I was scheduled to have minor surgery three days after Al died, and I was trying to think whether that was a good idea or not (which shows how poorly my brain was functioning), only to find that Lauren had already called and postponed it. She was *amazing*! I was so grateful.

Local friends helped finalize the service details, print a program, and pull together a worship team. Al's family from Florida came and nearly froze in the bitter cold weather we had that week, especially at the burial, so a woman from church rounded up coats for them and another dropped off a space heater. Al's family helped collect pictures of him for a slide show. Our friend Sinclair cut short a speaking engagement to give the homily at the memorial service, and our friend Karyn set up the technology to live stream it for those who could not come. A new committee from our church had been formed to host receptions for funerals, and the poor members' maiden voyage was to provide and serve food for a thousand guests at Al's service. A band of friends came back to our house after the service and prepared a warm, comforting meal for all of our relatives to come home to, including all of my sisters who had traveled a long distance. Faraway friends from every era of Al's life came from all over the country, and some of them stayed with folks from our church.

Al would have been bowled over by so many folks being part of the service. I kept wishing I could tell him about it. People meant so much to him, and he would have been over the moon if he could have visited with each one of them. We were incredibly blessed.

Al's burial was on Friday, and the day was frigid. Dear friends stood in the icy, fierce cold to commit his body to the earth. We knew that the burial would be both sad and joyful, probably with sadness having the edge. It was wonderful, and contained the hope of the resurrection, but it was certainly also somber. The body that had served Al so well— the feet that ran mile records and the hands that shot baskets, wrote articles, and served us all—we committed to the earth with honor and dignity, ashes to ashes, dust to dust.

The memorial service was on Saturday. As one of the kids said, "The focus of the burial is more on the physical body and the death part of dying, but the emphasis of the memorial service is more on the joy of heaven and the eternal life part of dying." All week we looked forward to the memorial service on Saturday, and we were not disappointed! It was a wonderful, joy-filled celebration, where Al and Jesus were both honored, and we came away with hearts uplifted and full of thankfulness. All four of our kids, both of Al's brothers, and three of his friends shared recollections.

There had been and would be plenty of tears and aching hearts, but we knew it would warm our hearts to remember the service, a time of celebrating Jesus's costly victory and its benefits, which Al was enjoying. Having people there with us, whether in person or from around the world via the live stream, made the service a *community* celebration, and that was exactly what was so important to Al.

# 58

# A Letter from Home

A l wrote the following letter for his memorial service:

As I have walked through the valley of the shadow of death, I have walked hand in hand with Jesus, the One who has already walked through that valley and come out the other side, alive, raised from the dead. And as I hold his hand and trust him, I too am raised with him, for this was his purpose in walking that path: to raise those who trusted in him. His rod and staff, his cross of suffering have become my comfort. Now as I have died, I come before God, the King of the universe, and I come in Christ. He chose to suffer and die on the cross in my place, so that on account of him I might have forgiveness from sin and victory over death. And now I have received the resurrection and eternal life that has been my only hope, past, present, and forever.

I have led a truly blessed life. At a young age, I realized that Jesus was not just a story in a comic book, but that he was real and I could actually know him. I wish I could describe to you what a powerful moment of understanding that was, and I have thought about it many times over the years, marveling over and over at the truth of this central fact. The Lord placed me into the perfect family where I was raised by loving parents with wonderful siblings. God gave me a wonderful wife who has been my joy as we have raised four wonderful children together. The Lord has given me the opportunity to be intimately involved in the lives of so many wonderful brothers and sisters, in our fellowship at college, as a pastor in Vermont, as an elder at New Life Church, and as a professor at

Westminster Seminary. Through family and ministry, I have had the privilege of loving and being loved by all of you, and I have been struck again and again by the deposit that each of you has left in my life.

Through all my life, Christ has been constant. Even as I have grown and changed, he is still the One whom I loved that first day. And nothing ever changed in how I came to him; every day of my life the story is the same: I come to God in Christ. His love for me has been steadfast, and he has pursued me through every time I have turned away from him and every time I have returned. The constant prayer of my heart for my own life and the lives of those around me has been that we would see Jesus, and that he would be welcome and present among us.

There may be some here who have never trusted Christ for life, who have never known that he is the answer to the sin and death in our lives. I urge you to consider the claims he made to being the Son of God, to consider that he didn't stay dead and sends a message down through the ages that there is life in him and him alone. His death on a cross, humiliating though it seemed, was his glory, by which he has defeated our true enemies—sin and death. By the ultimate sacrifice he made, he humiliated all powers arrayed against him.

If you struggle with faith, let me encourage you that in the hardest moments I have faced, he has been there. And death has been defeated. I am in Christ, as you are in Christ. So let us live out of the grace we have received. Let us live out of Christ. This means looking daily for him, asking him to open your eyes to him, and embracing what you see. Seek him with all your heart. Love him with all your heart. Love those he loves with all your heart, even to the laying down of your life for him. Jesus, the way, the truth, the life. In no other do we have hope. But in him we have hope that endures forever. We grieve, but we grieve with hope. The hope of a resurrection; the hope of life eternal. Together with Jesus.

For most of my Christian life I have wanted to see Jesus face-to-face, to join in with the heavenly chorus in his presence around his royal throne and declare his praise in new ways. Something else has grown through the years—an abiding sense that this is not for me alone. Being with Jesus by myself is not what he wants nor is it what I want. To be there with you all, those he loves and those

I have come to love, that is true joy. I have often thought of coming to heaven with Jesus standing at the finish line of a race awaiting those looking for him, trusting in him, pursuing him. But it isn't a race for me to finish first or alone. It has always been a race for us to finish together, arm in arm, having encouraged one another in faith.

He is good. From the beginning, his steadfast love has endured. It endures forever. He is a gracious God, slow to anger, abounding in steadfast love. Trust in him with all your heart, for he is faithful.

# 59

## God's Good Timing

The day Al died, laboring to breathe hour after hour, we wondered why the Lord waited so long to take him. I don't mean that we railed against his judgment or questioned his wisdom; I think the Lord granted us all peace to trust that he knew what he was doing and that he was doing it in love. But we were curious as to what purpose was being served by making Al wait so long.

In the next week I began to discern an answer. I think it was for us.

We had had such a wonderful time with Al during his last week that once he lost consciousness, we longed for him to be free. For ten hours on that Monday as he labored to breathe, every one of us ached for him to be released. That was all we yearned for hour after hour. When you have to wait for something you really want with all your heart, whether it's getting your first bicycle or having children after struggling with infertility, receiving that desire is an exquisite joy. Because we had to wait with increasing longing for Al's release, any other emotions—like regret, or wishing to prolong the time or to hang on—were burned away, and seeing Al finally set free was a moment of nothing but celebration. In the midst of such great sorrow at losing our husband and dad, what more wonderful gift than to see that moment transformed into joy?

The week after Al died, the memory of the moment of his passing was so precious. Knowing that we had all had the chances we needed to say goodbye, and knowing that we would not have wanted it to last any longer, brought such peace to our hearts. The protracted time we had and the resultant joy we experienced at Al's passing actually turned out to make the subsequent days easier. I wouldn't have anticipated that, but the Lord knew it. He asked Al to do one last thing for his family—to wait in the valley of the shadow of death for an extended period before being able to come out the other side into the glorious light of heaven. If it had been up to us, we would have chosen for the Lord to take Al quickly. If it had been up to Al, even though he was so eager to be with Jesus, he would have chosen to wait, if that would help us. Thankfully, it was neither his choice nor ours, and the Lord knew best.

God's choices are sometimes hard to figure out. Some we will never understand on this side of the grave. But sometimes we can see the wisdom in retrospect, and this was one of those times. We could actually see why what seemed like a bad thing (Al having to linger) was in fact a blessing (because our desire for his release made his passing a moment of joy rather than sorrow). We knew there would be times ahead when we might ask God why he gave Al only fifty-four years. It was good to have the reminder at *that* moment, *tied right into Al's death*, that God's ways and wisdom are far above ours. They are always best and always for our blessing.

# 60

## A Particular Mercy

I am immensely grateful that while Al was dying, he remained himself right up to the end.

In May of 2006, when the first tumor in Al's brain was discovered, the doctors and nurses asked us if we had noticed any personality changes because of the location of the tumor. All of us dreaded the thought of him becoming totally different from the gentle, loving, compassionate man he had always been. He dreaded that thought most of all. He did not want to be remembered by his children as someone cantankerous, vulgar, or vicious.

But he remained completely himself—gracious, patient, loving, and enjoying people—literally up to the point when he lost consciousness. Four days before he died he became spatially disoriented, so that after a trip to the bathroom he didn't know which room he was supposed to go back to or how to get there. Three days before he died, he was unable to get out of bed and didn't know how to find the cup of water at his bedside. But even the following day, when he had little strength to talk, he still knew every person he saw just as sharply as he ever had, and he interacted with them with obvious pleasure. Forty-eight hours before he died, we had a room full of recent college grads singing around his bed, and he pushed through his mumbled speech to say to those he knew, "How do you like Boston?"

"Congratulations on your wedding."

"How's engineering?"

And he made sure he learned the names of the new faces.

That was Al. Right to the very, very end, he was Al.

# LIFE AFTER

# 61

## Invisible Wounds

In the first weeks after Al died, the awareness of his absence colored all my thoughts, my feelings, my dreams, my outlook on the world. Even when I was not specifically thinking about it, it was always there in the background. It was like acting in a play with a large, three-dimensional mountain taking up most of the stage. You might not always be looking at it or interacting with it, but it's always there, affecting what you can and can't do, dominating the scene.

Sometimes Al's death seemed surreal. We found ourselves thinking, "He's just resting."

"He's just on the computer in the other room."

"He's away on a trip."

At other times his absence felt very real. It hit in the little, insignificant aspects of daily life. The first time I went to the grocery store after he died, I reached for the foods he loved and then realized he wasn't here to eat them anymore and never would be again. I felt as if someone had punched me in the gut right there in the popcorn aisle. When something happened that Al would have been especially interested in—a note someone wrote on a card that Al would have been touched by, for instance—I instinctively thought, *Oh, that's so nice. I'll have to tell Al*, and then I realized that I couldn't.

I was picking the raw onions off my Whopper and realized, *Al is not here to eat my onions, or the mushrooms off the kids' pizza or the other leftovers on our plates.*

It felt odd that the reality of Al's death was not patently obvious to everyone I came into contact with. I felt as if I had lost a leg or had half my face burned away; surely my loss was as visible on the outside as it was on the inside. Yet when I was pumping gas or grocery shopping, strangers around me were totally unaware of the ache in my chest or that anything was amiss.

It was thus a blessing to live among lots of people who had known and loved Al and who were also grieving his loss. That fellowship of grief was an enormous balm to our souls. I felt so badly for Al's mom and dad, who were not surrounded by a community who had known Al. I'm sure folks were sympathetic enough upon hearing, "Our son just died," but sympathy for an unknown stranger can only go so far.

We felt the Lord's faithfulness and goodness to all of us, and we knew his nearness. We walked one day at a time, trusting that the Lord would work everything out. There were laughter and tears, often inter-mixed, and a deep thankfulness for each other and for the many people around us who loved us and held us up.

We gradually discovered the truth that there is no shortcut through grief, no "efficient" way to minimize its pain. If there is a temporary way "around" it, taking that path is unwise. It only postpones hav-ing to eventually, inevitably deal with the pain. We just had to walk through it. So we did, one day at a time.

And the Lord walked with us.

# 62

## Bumps in the Road

In the first few months after Al died, I ran into some minor—and not so minor—logistical bumps.

For example, the bank account we wrote checks on and that our credit card was tied to was a joint account. In 2006 I had checked to see if I needed to do anything with it in preparation for Al's death, and they said no, it should be fine. When the time came, however, it turned out that since Al's Social Security number was the primary one on the account, it was not actually fine for me to access those funds. I wish they had told me that when I called.

That was just one example. At one point there were so many glitches like that, all clustered in such ridiculous concentration, that it became almost as comical as it was frustrating.

But it was good for me to have to deal with those challenges. It forced me to (1) trust God to sort out the snarls, hopefully each one before it had a chance to compound the next, (2) find out that I could in fact learn to organize and handle the financial, business, and administrative details of life that had never been my strong suit, even when they were out of the ordinary and a bit complicated, and (3) know that we had a myriad of friends with an array of skills who could help me if I needed it.

God didn't expect me to be able to do everything perfectly, so I slowly realized that I shouldn't expect it either. I had to feel my way and sometimes learn by trial and error, and that was okay. What God really wanted was for me to trust him, to walk with him, and to do my best. And with his help I *could* eventually learn to do what I needed to, even if it took some time.

I certainly grew stronger in the midst of it, which was a good thing. And thankfully, Al had life insurance, so he provided a cushion for us even after he was gone.

# 63

## Grief and Hope

All the while, we thought constantly about the incredible life Al was enjoying in heaven. Knowing that he was there with the Lord he loved so dearly and that we would see him again made an enormous difference. Al was drinking in the pure air of heaven, walking in the light that comes from God rather than from the sun, rejoining people he loved or meeting ones he never knew in this world, and exploring wonders that the most breathtakingly beautiful things on this earth only poorly mirror. Sometimes I would even picture Al running over the hills of heaven with indescribable life and health pounding through his being, or perhaps playing basketball, which he had always referred to as "nature's perfect sport." Some aspects of what I was picturing will come with the final consummation, when our bodies will be resurrected, but I knew for sure that Al was worshiping the Lord face-to-face, surrounded by God's people from all of history. I couldn't even imagine the glory of it. We all wished we could be flies on the wall when Al and his beloved Isaiah sat down to talk.

When Al and I were dating, we liked to sing a song from Psalm 27:4, which says, "One thing have I desired of the LORD, that will I seek after; that I may dwell in the house of the LORD all the days of my life, to behold the beauty of the LORD, and to enquire in his temple" (KJV). It's the only song I remember Al harmonizing to, and the harmony he sang was beautiful. Now I knew that was where he was at last and that he was deeply satisfied and content. Since the Lord had tapped him to jump ahead into the business of living Real Life, I couldn't wish him back here.

It reminded me quite a bit of when Alasdair went away to college. I had spent two years bracing myself for how much I was going to miss him and how sad I was going to be. But when we dropped him off at college and saw how happy he was there, how well he fit, and how obvious it was that he was exactly where he should be and wanted to be and where he would thrive, I couldn't really be sad. I missed him, but knowing how happy he was made my heart glad rather than sad. It was that way with Al too. We missed him terribly, but knowing the incredible joys he was experiencing, we were so happy for him that it helped to counterbalance our sadness and pain.

As Al had reminded us, it is not wrong to grieve. But we grieve with hope (1 Thessalonians 4:13). We *grieve* because in this fallen world death takes every person, but that is not the way God intended the world to be! There was no death until Adam and Eve sinned and broke the whole creation. Jesus grieved. He wept at a friend's tomb (John 11:35). But we grieve *with hope* because Jesus conquered death and set his people free from it (Isaiah 25:7–8; Hebrews 2:14–15). That takes the sting out of death (1 Corinthians 15:54–55) and gives us a sure and certain hope, now and for the future (1 Peter 1; Romans 8:18).

Those promises were keenly, intensely, personally precious to us in the months after Al died. They are always precious, of course, but during that time we *knew* them with a rock-solid certainty that brought an immense comfort to our hearts.

# 64

## A Borrowed Picture

I later discovered that a friend Al had met at the gym, Tim Eimer, had done a lot of thinking about heaven, and that the way he pictured it was very similar to my picture. Again, it may be that what we are imagining will not take place until the end of history in the new heavens and new earth. But Tim put it so beautifully that I asked him if I could include one of his descriptions in this book. He graciously gave permission. His description follows:

> As for me, I fix my gaze on heaven as I wait. Near my school, I run in a beautiful, wooded valley laced with trails winding their way along clear streams and through thick trees. Even this precious place has grown dim for me, a mere shadow of its heavenly counterpart, but at night, I daydream about heaven like a boy dreaming about playing professional baseball. I imagine running with a body now swift and strong. Golden hair streams behind me and my muscles explode with power. Sometimes I run alone; at other times I'm with many of you, and we shine with radiant beauty for we are now part of Christ's glory (John 17:1). We sprint between trees as thick as houses with roots that plunge down into the very spine of the mountains. Fearless, we plunge into clear, green pools teeming with fish of every kind, and we dive down deep to explore the mysteries hidden in the depths. We run the trails again in perfect harmony, knowing that nothing can hurt us or separate us from

the joy of being together. Narnian creatures greet us from the trees, and we shout in reply. In tree houses created by craftsmen more talented than the Renaissance geniuses, we pause to drink wine from God's very own vineyard and toast our allegiance to our Lord and King. Laughter streams from our lips in celebration of a fellowship so deep and intimate that we cannot imagine how we survived on such impoverished friendships back on the old earth. We race on, gathering others as we go, toward the great capital city of our heavenly country, for tonight the King has prepared a banquet for his citizens.

Ahhh. I, for one, can't wait!

# 65

## No Time to Grieve

One of the benefits of coming face-to-face with death is that it shows you how important certain things are and how unimportant others are. The problem with that, at least if you are in high school, is that when you're weighing the eternal value of things, it can be tough to get excited about trigonometry or literary criticism.

Eowyn found it difficult to engage with her courses as Al's cancer progressed. Not surprisingly, that situation reached critical levels around the time of his death. The week before Al died, she was physically present in school but unable to concentrate, and definitely not working on long-term assignments. Then she missed two weeks completely, and the first two weeks she was back in school she had no emotional energy to dive into schoolwork. She made as much effort as she could to attempt some of the assignments of those two weeks, but she kept falling further and further behind. So by the middle of March, she basically had a five-week slide to reverse. That was so discouraging that it was disabling, and the more the work piled up, the more discouraged she became. You know how those downward spirals go.

It felt like a no-win situation. Eowyn needed time to grieve. I knew it was important for her to do that. In fact, I believed that grieving was by far the most important thing for her to do at that point, and if I could have, I would have stopped the world and let her grieve at her own speed without thinking about schoolwork. But I also knew that the longer she waited to start tackling that mountain of work the further behind she would get, and the harder it would be to ever get out from under the pile. Already, concepts she had missed in trig and chemistry were critical to the content they were currently covering, so she was feeling increasingly lost. We talked about the possibility of just forgetting it and repeating tenth grade, but that wasn't what she wanted, and we both knew it. In our society very little time is allowed for grieving before you are expected to jump back into work or school and carry on as if everything were normal.

We were in touch with her guidance counselor and teachers about making up work, and they were helpful. Someone told us about a grief support group for kids, but neither Eowyn nor Alden wanted to go, and I didn't force them. (I've heard many adults say that the support group GriefShare was helpful to them.)

Eowyn and I mapped out a plan to chip away at the pile in manageable chunks, and she made bits of progress in getting some assignments handed in, tests taken, etc. Every little bit helped. I tried hard to discern the line between giving her lots of space and holding her to the schedule we had laid out. She tried hard to remember that I was doing that for her sake. It was tough all around.

Then Anne, the wife of one of our pastors, who had a great relationship with Eowyn, told her, "I'd be glad to come over and sit with you while you work. I can help you learn things if you want, or I can just be with you for companionship—a warm body in the same room while you study." That was fantastic. It kept holding to a schedule from becoming a problem between Eowyn and me and gave her the encouragement she needed to keep pushing forward and not give up. To this day I get misty-eyed remembering that gift. Anne had a busy life with a job, a husband who was a pastor, and three kids of her own, but she was willing to be Jesus to Eowyn and help her get through an impossible-feeling patch. *That* is the body of Christ at its best.

# 66

## Alone in the Crowd

Alden grieved differently. He kept up with school assignments, but the social scene was tough. His first day back at school one girl asked him, "So what's it like now that your dad isn't there anymore?" Ouch. He didn't know who knew that he'd just lost his dad and who didn't. If people weren't saying anything about it, was it because they didn't know, or because they weren't sure what to say, or because they didn't care? Should he talk about it or keep quiet? Did he really even want to think about it or could he shut it out of his mind? Hard waters to navigate at thirteen.

Both Eowyn and Alden were being brave about doing what they had to in the midst of deep grief. Yet I remember a day in the first weeks after Al died when Eowyn was having such a hard time emotionally that I decided to let her stay home from school. Alden seemed about the same as every other day, so I was getting ready to send him off to the bus as usual. But when he found out that Eowyn was staying home, his backpack dropped out of his hand, he burst into tears, and he stood in the middle of the kitchen, arms at his sides, sobbing. I hadn't realized how close to the ragged edge his emotions were running. Needless to say, he stayed home too. I skipped my class, and we all had a snug, low-stress day at home together, letting our clenched hearts relax a bit.

Alden's social studies teacher, Mr. Robinson, was a gem, and Alden absolutely loved him, as had Eowyn two years earlier. A month or so after Al died, Mr. Robinson took a position as an assistant principal at another school. We were glad for the great opportunity for him, but it was another significant loss for Alden right on the heels of Al's death.

Junior high is a hard world to survive in even if you haven't just lost your dad. You're trying to figure out who you really are and who you want to be, and all the while the pressure to be cool is enormous. Most of the time you feel like a nobody, and then if someone starts to think you're somebody, it goes straight to your head. Alden didn't talk a lot about what he was thinking or feeling, but it was clear that he was struggling with grief, and with life, and with himself. Not surprisingly, that created challenges for all of us. Alden wasn't "getting into trouble," but it distressed me to see him unhappy when I wasn't able to help him.

That summer, the family of one of his good school friends, Pablo, generously invited him to go to Spain with them when they visited Pablo's grandparents. Another friend, Tim, and his family took him with them to vacation in Maine. We were so touched. Alden's heart was still fragile enough that I didn't know whether he would be able to do either of those things, but they turned out to be wonderful times and good steps in the healing process.

# 67

# Humbling Love

Our friends Charles and Anne reminded us one day that it is important for people who are suffering to know they are loved. We certainly knew throughout Al's journey that we were loved—by God and by people.

Throughout the year Al was dying and beyond, we were loved beyond all imagination, not only by God directly—through his Holy Spirit and his Word—but by his people. What we received was vastly beyond anything we deserved and was deeply humbling. It's the kind of thing that is so overwhelming, so gracious, so unmerited, so far beyond measure, that it makes you just bow your head in grateful silence. There are no words that are an adequate response to such love. I could not possibly mention every gesture of love that people gave to us during Al's last year because it would fill this entire book. But I will share a sampling.

We received so many meals that we lost count. Jeff, a seminary student, cooked dinner for us every Tuesday for months and months, and his meals were yummy! Bill, a family friend from church, cooked for us repeatedly even though he himself undergoes repeated back surgeries. When we had a large group of company from out of town, my friend Peggy brought breakfast trays and other goodies and hired someone to clean my house beforehand.

My friend Susan came on more than one occasion to "steal" our laundry and return it washed, dried, and folded. Friends from church came and did yard work and planted flowers, and the junior high youth group helped us move things out of our garage, which had to be torn down. When Al's feet were blistered so that he couldn't walk, seminary students came and moved our bed out of the loft where we slept and helped shift Al's office around. Al's brother came from Florida and fixed all kinds of broken things around the house.

People showered us with gifts large and small, from flowers and soft towels that would feel comforting to Al, to a "real" TV (to replace our teeny old one). One day our friend Frank showed up in my kitchen and declared that he and Roland were going to replace our countertops! My sister Abby sent me a warm, soft, fuzzy bathrobe to remind me of God's loving arms around me (I still think of her and of God's love every time I wear it). And on Thanksgiving Day, our auto mechanic Mark showed up with an apple pie that he himself had baked!

People visited us from far away. They sent cards and wrote unbelievably encouraging comments on our blog. They prayed for us. The parents of one of Alden's school friends offered prayers for Al in their synagogue. Marc detoured on his way home from work during Al's last weeks to sit in his car outside our house and pray for us. Folks loved, supported, listened to, and prayed for our kids, which was *priceless*.

The week Al died, Doug went and picked up hospice medications for us, and Tina dropped off gorgeous flowers and a worship CD to cheer us around Al's bed. Karyn brought over trays of healthy things for us to snack on, since we weren't eating meals, and Jim dropped off a machine to freshen the air in Al's room because it was too cold to open the windows.

Our medical professionals were outstanding and went above and beyond the call of duty.

The list could go on and on. Dozens and dozens more people could be named, whose love and care were every bit as precious to us. The love we experienced from start to finish was staggering, and I cannot begin to put into words what a difference that made. Those people were the hands and feet of Jesus loving us, and through them he was with us—tangibly and unmistakably. *God was here.*

God meets each individual in grief, and he does so in many different ways. He may meet grieving people in ways that differ from those we experienced. Often he shows his love through people, but if someone is alone, he may manifest his love through his Holy Spirit alone, who is sufficient to comfort, strengthen, and sustain. This much I know: in whatever fashion, *he will be there.*

# 68

## Living with Sadness and Hope

Suffering is real, and painful, and life-changing, and we shouldn't minimize that. The good news of Jesus's triumph over death and sin is real, and hope-filled, and life-changing, and we shouldn't minimize that either. We have to hold both truths in our hands at the same time and walk a line between them without falling off on either side.

I think that initially I fell off on the side of thinking I could minimize the pain for my kids. They had lost their father and that was terribly sad. Of course, I knew that. But because the gospel brings so much hope, and probably because I am a "fixer" by nature, I guess I thought that if I could just "do everything right" as a parent, I could somehow cushion my kids from a lot of the pain of grief. If I could be loving enough, patient enough, encouraging enough, and strong enough, and if I could support them in just the right way, they wouldn't hurt too badly. I could somehow make up for their loss and make everything somewhat okay.

But the truth finally came home to me one day that this was impossible. I could never be both parents to them. I could never make up for the loss of their dad. He was gone, and no amount of good parenting on my part was going to fill that void. The pain and grief of his absence were facts I couldn't change—could hardly even touch in fact.

Rebeckah has commented, "Losing someone you love is like losing an arm. If you lose a limb, you learn how to cope, how to compensate, how to do life one-armed, how to carry on. Eventually the new state of affairs even starts to feel somewhat normal. *But you are still missing an arm.*" She's absolutely right.

I suppose we often fall off on the other side too, minimizing the hope of the gospel—the good news about Jesus triumphing over death, setting us free from its power, and making us part of his family. That good news does a lot to undo the sadness of suffering in specific, tangible ways in specific, real-life situations.

For us, the gospel took the sting out of death. It did so for Al because when he died, he began to really *live* in God's presence, full of joy, wholeness, and wonder. And it did so for the rest of us because we knew where Al was and could delight in the joys he was experiencing. We also knew we would someday be together with him again.

I also knew that the Lord would be a father to my children. Because of his covenant promises throughout the Bible, he would always be with them, listen to them, guide them, comfort them, strengthen them, and encourage them. He would never die and leave them, as Al had had to do. The Bible is *full* of God's care for the fatherless, so I knew he would watch over them, provide for their needs, and protect them.

And the gospel gave us a second family. Our own family is wonderful, and I'm so thankful for the way they loved and supported us, even from far away. Because of the gospel, we had another family nearby too—the church. We had people who grieved with us, prayed for us, and helped us with all kinds of practical things. Although their dad was gone, my kids would be around men who would love them and show them what it looks like to live as men of faith and faithfulness.

The benefits of Jesus's death and resurrection were real and brought genuine relief and blessing. The gospel doesn't necessarily alter the circumstances of suffering in our lives. Suffering is real and painful, and it may continue to be painful for a long, long time. The gospel didn't change the fact that my children were still without their dad. Al was gone, and he wasn't coming back. I couldn't erase the pain and grief of that for my kids. But the gospel does set our suffering in the context of a bigger reality—that Jesus came to reverse the curse of sin and death, and *already* his victory is turning back its effects. One day sin and death will be entirely eradicated, and as his people we long for that day, but *even now* we experience a foretaste of it. Even now that reality brings hope in so many ways (1 Thessalonians 4:13).

We cannot always "fix" situations or alleviate people's hardships. But we can pray that God will give them eyes to see and inhabit the bigger picture—the truer reality—and find hope, relief, peace, comfort, blessing, strength, and even joy in the midst of hardships.

# 69

## How Do You Keep Warm?

In our journey through Al's cancer, people sometimes commented that our family was strong or inspiring. I can testify in complete honesty, without a shred of doubt, that whatever strength we had came from God. We were extremely ordinary people with an extraordinary God sustaining us. *He* made all the difference.

Consider three images.

First, picture a bitter, cold, wintry scene. Picture a guy in shorts and a T-shirt standing in the pelting snow and icy wind. I don't mean high school kids who go without coats to be "cool" but someone like our friend Eric, who wears shorts and a T-shirt all winter—even skiing!—because the cold genuinely doesn't bother him. Eric's tolerance for cold is amazing. We were not like Eric. We were ordinary people who felt the cold of loss and sorrow like anyone else.

Next, picture our frigid house, which has forced hot air heat that blows out of air vents in the floor. Picture a guy in shorts and a T-shirt standing over the vent while the hot air is blowing, feeling warm enough to be comfortable until it shuts off. Someone looking in the window who couldn't see the vent might think that person was like Eric, but we would know that he was warm only because of the hot air blowing around him. We were a lot more like that. Apparently, looking at us from the outside, some people may have thought we were somehow impervious to the devastation of grief. Maybe they couldn't see the "heater" of God's steadfast love sustaining us, but it was most certainly the only reason we were not undone by the cold of loss.

Finally, imagine a beach in Hawaii, 75 to 80 degrees every day with full sunshine. Picture a guy in shorts and a T-shirt, relaxing comfortably in the balmy warmth. He doesn't have to figure out how to get warm; he simply inhabits a warm reality. This is probably the truest picture of what Jesus brought about for his people. We humans broke God's beautiful creation and brought death into it, but when Jesus died and rose again 2,000 years ago, he destroyed the power of death and created a whole new reality for his people to live in. That reality includes eternity, with our brief lives in this world as a split-second prelude to it and death as its door. When you look forward to the unimaginable joys of heaven, it changes everything. It changes life here.

The Lord was kind enough to give us eyes to see what was already the case. In our sadness, what we needed most was simply a reminder and an awareness that the wonderful eternal life Jesus bought with his blood was ours and Al's. In that awareness, our grief could ease and our souls could relax, as we found ourselves in the warmth and comfort of the sure hope of heaven. It was like stepping out of the bitter cold winter and onto the sunny, Hawaiian beach. We certainly didn't manage to live in the spiritual reality of that beach all the time—in fact, we frequently didn't. But when we missed Al and felt the deep cold in our hearts, what brought healing warmth was the sure knowledge of heaven—that Al was there with Jesus in full health and joy and that we would see him again. That is what sustained us.

# 70

# Waiting for Christopher Robin

When Al died, I was still working on a master's degree at Westminster. He died right at the start of the spring semester (in fact, classes were canceled the next day), and during that semester I would sometimes do my schoolwork in his office.

Al had worked so much in that office. It held papers and notes that were the product of his mind and energies over decades. He had read and loved and drawn from the books on the shelves. They were his love as well as his livelihood. With their help he had brought forth words and ideas that fed and equipped seminary students, that taught them God's Word, and that challenged and inspired them to take the good news of God's *shalom* to the ends of the earth. Al and those books had been partners in a great endeavor. Now the books sat on the shelves, abandoned and mute. Their partner was gone. I could almost imagine that they missed him.

I thought of baby birds in a nest, waiting for their mother to return. Or Winnie the Pooh waiting for Christopher Robin to come back and play. But mother birds sometimes get killed, and the baby birds go on waiting, not understanding why their mother doesn't return. Christopher Robin grew up and left Pooh behind. In Al's office, I imagined the books were waiting for their friend to walk back in and pick up where he and they had left off. But he wasn't ever coming back. It made me sad.

Psalm 103:15–16 says, "As for man, his days are like grass; he flourishes like a flower of the field; for the wind passes over it, and it is gone, and its place knows it no more." But this felt a bit like the opposite, almost like Al's "place" remembering him.

Of course, books don't have feelings. I know that. Nor am I contradicting Scripture. The point of that verse is to reflect on the temporariness of our life on this earth in contrast to God's steadfast love, and that is absolutely true. It was true for Al as it is for all of us; his life here was short.

But the Bible also talks about the inheritance a good man leaves behind. Al liked to talk about the deposits that various people had made in his life. He certainly left a deposit in the lives of many others. His impact on so many people—students, friends, family, colleagues—still continues in this world. "His place" (not his books, but the people he touched) may still know him for a while longer, and for that I am grateful.

Alasdair and I each kept quite a few of Al's books, and the remainder we sent with international students who were going home to places that don't have such resources. I think Al would have been happy about that. I hope the books will continue to be fruitful in the hands of other partners for years to come.

# 71

# Light on My Face

Over the course of Al's battle with cancer and in the years since, a number of things have struck me about worship.

Sometimes we sing songs that express how much we love God. During periods when I am excited about him, those are great. But when I feel dry or cold or distant or weary, those songs feel hollow at best and sometimes even hypocritical to sing.

But songs that talk about God's love for *us* are always something I can sink my teeth into. They remind me that God's love for me isn't based on whether I'm feeling warm or cold toward him; it's based on what he has done for me. He loved us enough to send his Son to rescue us, and that Son intentionally gave up his life so that we could be restored. That is something objective, something that actually happened at a point in history. It's not trapped in the little subjective world of how I feel; it is part of a vastly bigger reality. It is a truth that is firm and secure apart from how I feel on any given day. I can look back and see God's faithfulness to his people through human history and to me personally over more than four decades.

Some worship songs have to do with the challenges of life on earth, or with God's faithfulness to us during suffering, or with a call to persevere and to serve him with joy, or with the blessings of companionship as we journey together, or other things pertaining to the Christian life. Those songs are great, encouraging, and important, but they are like flying below the clouds.

But ahh . . . other worship songs break through those clouds and lift you right into the heavenly throne room. By faith you see God in his majesty, reigning in glory, Almighty and Ancient of Days, all-powerful and all-loving. You see Jesus, willingly humbled and slain for us, but raised in glory and seated at the Father's right hand, extending his kingdom of love and blessing into all the earth. When I sing those songs, I feel the heavenly light on my face, and I join in worship with a throng of brothers and sisters—not only those who are physically in the room with me, but with the church worldwide and also with those who have died and who now worship the Lord face-to-face.

At those moments in my imagination, I feel as if I can *almost* see those others and if I could just peer around, I might glimpse Al's face in the crowd. It's almost like being together with him in the same place at the same time, since we are both before God's throne—he in actuality and I by faith. Someday we will be there together. And in the meantime it is a privilege, a joy, and a sweet refreshment to stand by faith in the radiance of God's presence, to close my eyes and feel the light of his glory on my face.

# 72

## Just a Blink

In the months after Al died, heaven seemed very close, not only spatially, but also temporally.

Before that time, the "someday" nature of heaven always had an element of far-distant future to it, maybe because it is the start of eternity, and eternity by its very nature seems a long way off. But what I began to see and marvel at was that *in the present moment*, Al was there enjoying heaven. That struck me with new force and clarity. For each of us, heaven could be only a breath away. Even if we live another fifty or 100 years, that sort of time span suddenly seemed wonderfully short, with the joy of heaven right around the corner. It felt like the last few months of a long engagement. When you hit the homestretch, the waiting takes on a different character. The wedding seems suddenly real in a way it didn't before. I realized, heaven will come soon! Just as a year seems to fly by faster and faster the older I get, I suddenly saw that the time until our arrival in heaven was as nothing. Even now, we're almost there.

At one point I had conversations with two different people who knew they were likely to die in the near future. As I talked with each of them, it was clear that they both were living with a calm awareness that their days were few. Barring a miracle, their graduation to glory would likely come soon. They both knew that the greatest miracle had already happened—2,000 years ago in Palestine—and that because of it they had nothing to fear in death, only a glorious expectation of much greater life ahead. Our friend Sinclair commented to me that on the occasions when he saw Al during the year he was dying, it felt like waiting in an anteroom with someone who was about to have an audience with the Queen.

I began to see life as more of a continuum, like one of those moving walkways they have at airports. Somewhere along the walkway, suspended from the ceiling, was a thin barrier—like the bead curtains of the 1960s—that represented death, and each of us would pass through it at a certain time. We were all at different points along the moving walkway: I was alive here, maybe far away from the barrier. The two friends I mentioned were alive here, but just barely this side of the bead curtain; they would be in heaven shortly. Al was just barely on the other side of the curtain, only having been in heaven a short while. And many others had passed through it long ago and were far down the walkway.

I still felt closely connected to Al, even though he was on the other side. And somehow, talking to folks who knew they would soon step through the curtain into heaven made it seem very near. Life here is nothing more than a blink, and then we will be there.

# 73

## Sorting

Some people are pack rats. I am one of them, and Al was too. Our house was perfectly livable, not like something you would see on a TV show about hoarders, but it held *a lot* of stuff—especially Al's home office. The summer after Al died, I needed to sort through his things. So I asked the Lord to help me tackle it.

As it happened, the Lord sent help I would never have anticipated, in the form of my friend Jayne. She was between jobs at the time and has an absolute gift for organizing. She was incredibly generous with her time and came over every day of a week that Eowyn and Alden were away. What we accomplished in those five days was barely short of a miracle! During a second week when the kids were both away, we went at it again. Literally hundreds and hundreds and hundreds of pounds of stuff left our house. (Among them were dozens and dozens of Al's "to do" lists from which he was now gloriously free.) It is fair to say that she was a gift from God, and I would never have gotten through even a tenth of the project without her.

Next, Jayne and I assessed the state of Al's office at Westminster. Man, oh man, oh man. It was just one small room, but Al was a typical professor, and his office was overflowing with papers, files, and books. Just for my own curiosity, I measured the stuff that was in that little office. If we had stacked up the piles of papers that were not in file cabinets but were on top of things, under the chairs, etc., the pile would have been twelve and a half feet high. (One foot of stacked paper weighs about thirty pounds.) There were sixteen file drawers, all full, which would equal another thirty-two feet of papers if vertically stacked; seventy-five shelf-feet of books, plus ten more boxes of books; roughly twenty shelf-feet of journals; twenty-three stacking trays; office supplies; etc.

It wasn't just the sheer volume; each paper had to be individually handled and evaluated. The whole thing was totally overwhelming, and if I had been on my own I would have sat down, cried, and given up on the spot. But Jayne gave me the courage to begin, the encouragement to keep going, and great practical advice for evaluating files. We plowed through all the papers—in file drawers and not—and then all the office supplies and miscellaneous things. God bless her! I was *so* thankful for her company and help.

We then learned that Al had "some things" in a large storage closet in the basement. It turned out to be as much as was in his office! I was demoralized, but Jayne fortified me again with her unquenchable determination and enthusiasm, and we hauled out thirty-five more file boxes plus huge trash bags of stuff. Alasdair and I went through the books the next week, and after I had gone through lesser collections of things in two other spots on campus, the job was done.

Sorting through that much stuff at home and at Westminster was completely beyond me, but the Lord sent amazing help to carry me through. Once again I got to experience the body of Christ at its best. There is *no* doubt in my mind that Jayne was the visible, competent, strengthening hands and feet of Jesus to me that summer!

# 74

# Beauty in Broken Shells

The day before school started in September of 2007, I went to the beach with Eowyn, Alden, and Kristen (a good friend who had been the kids' youth group leader and who was then living with us). Kristen collects shells, and she said something there that stuck with me. She said she used to search for perfect, unbroken shells and rarely found them. Now she picks up broken shells and enjoys beautiful things about them—unusual colors, interesting shapes, and so on. She just made an offhand comment that maybe that's how life is: we want things to be perfect but they rarely are, and instead we can learn to look for and appreciate the surprising beauty God works into the broken world around us.

I think that is some of what happened for me, beginning with Al's diagnosis. Up until that time my life had seemed pretty close to perfect. I grew up in a wonderful family where I was loved, nurtured, and encouraged. I married an incredible man who loved me and with whom I shared a life blessed by God's love. We had four amazing children who were a phenomenal blessing to me. But as a result of Al's cancer and death, I have a slightly better picture—or at least a little glimpse—of the way most of humanity regularly experiences life. It's a rare person who gets to live a "perfect life."

Suffering is the norm on this planet; most people's lives have lots of brokenness in them, or they are worn down by the constant tossing of the waves. And yet God brings joy, blessings, beauty, and redemption into the brokenness. It is good to see and experience that—to feel pain and sadness and yet to see God's infinite, transforming grace in the midst of it, perhaps even more clearly for the contrast.

# 75

# What Do You Expect?

Eowyn and Alden definitely did *not* want to go back to school that fall after Al died. It's pretty standard not to want summer to end, yet to have an underlying excitement about seeing friends again, starting a new year, finding out who is in your classes, etc. But that year there was none of the latter sentiment. Not a trace. I think it was because the previous year had been so hard. We had been relieved to survive it and to stagger across the finish line into the reprieve of summer vacation. The thought of going back to the way things had been during the spring seemed about as appealing as a kick in the face. For Eowyn, knowing that the workload during junior year is extremely heavy didn't help. The spring had been grueling as she tried to dig out from under the pile of schoolwork that accumulated around the time Al died. The idea that the next year would be even worse was horrifying. However, even a demanding junior year would not be as bad as spring had been because she wouldn't be starting many weeks behind and trying to catch up.

As it turned out, the transition back to school went better than Eowyn and Alden had expected. They did have lots of homework and they were still doing school and life without their dad, but it was manageable and certainly better than the spring. Alden made the school soccer team, and Eowyn made the school play, neither of which were to be taken for granted. When we received those bits of good news, I realized something about the outlook on life we had come to hold.

A song we like to sing called "Blessed Be Your Name" by Matt Redman talks about two contrasting sets of circumstances: one full of blessings, sunshine, and abundance, and the other full of suffering, deserts, and difficulties. The song talks about blessing (praising) the name of the Lord in both sorts of times. During the year and a half since Al's diagnosis, we had done a lot of walking on the desert road, yet we had definitely seen God's love and tenderness in the midst of suffering. That was a deep blessing. As the school year started again, I think we subconsciously braced ourselves for more tough times, automatically assuming that life would be hard, challenging, and full of disappointments and sadness, but that we would know God's care in the midst of it. That had become our default assumption. When Alden made the soccer team and Eowyn got the title role in the play, I think we were all fairly astonished. The sunny road of abundant, happy blessing that we had walked on in years past had come to feel foreign to us. We had forgotten that life could be like that too.

I don't think there is inherent virtue in having a "default setting" for our expectations in either direction—assuming that life will be easy or assuming it will be difficult. If we expect God to give abundant, pleasant blessings all the time, that *could* be the result of a secure grasp of God's generosity, but it might also come from presumption and selfishness. On the other hand, if we expect God to send hardship and trials as daily fare, that *could* flow from an appreciation of the hidden blessing of growing closer to God in suffering (it may even feel "holy" somehow), but it might also stem from doubting his goodness. Neither default assumption is inherently right or wrong; either one can come from a good or bad heart attitude.

Rather than expecting either one and assuming we know what the Lord has in mind for us and why, I think he wants us to simply walk with him on whatever path he chooses for a given day or season. He wants us to be content to put our hand in his and trust him because he is the Lord, because he will bring into our lives what he alone knows is best, because he will walk the path with us, and because he has promised that ultimately he will turn every circumstance to our blessing and his glory.

# 76

# Trouble Sleeping

For a long time after Al died, I had trouble sleeping. I think that's fairly normal. I was so tired all the time that I could usually fall asleep pretty easily at night, but I would wake up at 4 or 5 a.m. (maybe because of the birds, during open-window weather). Within seconds, thoughts and worries would rush into my mind and fill it up, my heart would race with anxiety, and I would be unable to go back to sleep. There were so many details to stay on top of that I felt overwhelmed a lot of the time. When I discovered that I had dropped the ball on something important, it made me worry that there were other important balls out there somewhere that I had forgotten—or didn't even know about—that I was in danger of dropping too. They might be as simple as neglected phone calls or as complex as filing taxes or figuring out specific single-parenting questions.

Two Bible passages were a great help to me.

One was Psalm 3:5. David said, "I lay down and slept; I woke again, for the LORD sustained me." The setting for the psalm is David's flight from his son Absalom. David didn't know whether he would wake up at all or whether Absalom would find him during the night and kill him, yet he was able to lie down and sleep because he trusted in God's care for him. If God was so reliable that David could rest in him in such dire circumstances, and since I had seen God's even greater love shown in Jesus, then surely I could rest in him too.

The other passage was from Isaiah 40:11: "He will tend his flock like a shepherd; he will gather the lambs in his arms; he will carry them in his bosom, and gently lead those that are with young." I picture a shepherd carrying a little lamb, and the lamb relaxing in his strong arms and falling asleep.

After that—and still today—if I wake up at 5 a.m., I try to firmly head off the details that would like to storm into my mind. I choose to remember instead God's unfailing, trustworthy love and care. I picture myself as the little lamb being carried by the shepherd, even pretending that my mattress is his strong arms underneath me, and often I am able to drift back to sleep. Even if I remain awake, it's comforting to rest quietly in the Shepherd's strong arms.

# 77

# Just a Dream

Maybe you have come home after a relaxing vacation and found that, by the next week, the vacation seems as if it were a dream. Sometimes I've reflected on this phenomenon *while* on vacation. I have stopped and thought, *All these lovely surroundings are completely vivid and real right now, while home seems distant and unreal. But by next week when I am home, this place will have faded to a memory and will seem like a dream.* I think I have trouble taking seriously a reality that I am not presently experiencing.

During the year Al was dying, we knew there would be a time when he would be gone, but it didn't seem real. He and I planned for that future and discussed details of it. My head knew it made sense, but my heart couldn't grasp that there would be a time when he would really be gone.

The moment he died, that future began. At first, it seemed as if Al were still here, just in the other room resting, or away at work or on a trip. I think that's pretty normal; it's a form of denial that goes with the territory of grief. Gradually, we got used to the fact that he really was gone. And eventually, we settled into that new reality, and "the time before" while he was still with us felt increasingly like a dream.

Time rolled along and life happened without Al. Sometimes when we were reminiscing about events from the early months after Al died, we would forget that Al hadn't been here for them, and when we remembered, it would sort of surprise us. Only once, several years later, did I find myself thinking back on an event and being surprised to recall that Al *had* been part of it.

I think each of us has had dreams of Al since he died. When he is in my dreams, it always seems perfectly natural for him to be there. We are often involved in doing something very ordinary together, and I am unaware that there's anything odd about the fact that he's there. It's only once I wake up that I realize that this can only happen in my dreams, since he is not here anymore.

But there was one time that, even in my dream, I remembered he was dead and that the only reason he was present with me was that I was dreaming. In my dream, we were snuggling happily, as we used to do on the rare mornings that we didn't have to jump right out of bed and start the day. I was filling him in on what had been going on since he died. He, of course, wanted to hear about each of the kids and how they were doing. My dream seemed so real, so like one of those precious moments of life when he was still here.

In my dream, I was aware with keen regret that once I awakened, it would have been only a dream that would fade in the face of the day's activities. I said this to Al in the dream, and we both agreed that it was going to be very sad.

And it was. I cried a lot that day as I missed him.

# 78

## Surprise

Almost every year of the quarter century that Al taught at Westminster, he attended the annual meetings of the Society of Biblical Literature. SBL takes place somewhere in the US, always the Friday through Tuesday before Thanksgiving. Unfortunately, other things always happen that same weekend, including the fall play at our high school and the father-son camping weekend for the elementary school boys at our church. During the years that we had kids involved in one or the other of those activities, it was a challenge for Al to figure out how to be in two places at once. Of course he wanted to be here for the special activity of whichever child, but SBL was important enough for him to be genuinely torn. Sometimes he had to leave a day late for the meetings in order to catch the play, and one year Alasdair and his college roommate filled in for Al on Alden's father-son camping trip.

The fall after Al died, Eowyn had the title role in the school play. As I mentioned, that was a surprising blessing for her and a reminder that the Lord could put happy things in her life as well as hard ones. She felt very blessed, and we were all excited with and for her. It goes without saying that it was also going to be hard not to have Al there to see her perform. Life with grief is bittersweet, and the sweeter something is, the more bitter it is to experience it without your loved one. The play was going to be one of those reminders, and we knew that and accepted it.

What we didn't expect is that Al's friend and colleague Doug Green, who also always went to SBL, went a day late so that he could be there for Eowyn on opening night. We were speechless. We have been good friends with the Greens for years. Our kids call them Uncle Doug and Auntie Rose, our kids are friends with their kids, we have shared vacations and Christmas Eves. From the time Al died, Doug has filled a kind of older brother role to me and a close uncle role to the kids. But it never occurred to any of us that he would sacrifice part of SBL to be at Eowyn's play.

Sometimes God's love catches you by surprise.

# 79

## All the "Firsts"

It is generally accepted wisdom that the first year after someone's death is the hardest, and that is probably true. But I found that I didn't want to see that first year come to an end.

Each of the kids' birthdays that first year was tough. We were so painfully aware that Al was absent, that he would have loved to be there and wouldn't have wanted to miss their birthdays, that he loved them, that he wouldn't ever be there for their birthdays again.

I didn't know whether to buy them gifts "from Dad" or whether that would make it worse, so I made them each a T-shirt (which they could wear privately as pajamas if they wanted to) with a message from Al on it, using his unique, individual nickname for them. The Lord met us. For example, Eowyn's birthday was exactly one month—four weeks to the day—after Al died. The Lord showed his kindness through a friend of Eowyn and her mom, who threw a joint "Sweet Sixteen" party for Eowyn and her friend. I didn't have the emotional wherewithal to pull that together, but Linda did and she blessed Eowyn and took that job off my plate. What a provision.

Other holidays were hard as well. That year Father's Day happened to fall on Al's and my anniversary. Actually, it was probably good that two days that were going to be hard for the kids and for me happened on the same day. I asked the kids if they preferred to ignore Father's Day or to celebrate it, and they all chose to face and embrace it. So we ate good food, watched and discussed a movie Al would have enjoyed, and shared memories of Al that were funny, or poignant, or just dear to us. We were self-consciously and corporately thankful for Al, and it ended up being a good day together.

On Al's birthday we had a special meal and then went to a movie as a family, which was something Al loved to do. On Christmas the kids were all home, and we had a thoroughly relaxing day, staying in our pajamas and hanging out, which is our custom. It was good to be together.

As we approached the first anniversary of Al's death, someone commented that we must be relieved to see an end to all the "firsts" without Al. But I found that I didn't want to be done with the firsts. They were painful, but the acute pain of missing and remembering Al on each occasion had the effect of linking us intimately with him. It was like floating down a river passing signs marking "X amount of time since Al's death." The reminders of his absence were sad, but they still connected us to the event that initiated them—his death.

Once we reached the end of the firsts, we would leave the familiarity of the river and be propelled into the big, shoreless sea of "the rest of our lives." Sure, we would continue to mark time and to celebrate birthdays and holidays, but it would all be part of "life after Al" in a nebulous way that would stretch into countless years. That was a different kind of hard.

# 80

# Three Modes of Grief

During the year Al was dying and for a long time afterward, I found over and over again that there were three modes I seemed to operate in. (1) Sometimes I was simply busy doing life. (2) Sometimes I felt intense sorrow and grief as I missed Al. (3) Sometimes I was captivated by the hope and glory of heaven and the fact that Al was experiencing it.

These three modes wove in and out of my days in a haphazard fashion, especially in the year following Al's death. Often I could not predict or control which emotion would hit me at any given moment. Something completely unexpected might trigger grief that poured out in tears that I could not stop. But at other times, I could choose which mode to operate in.

I purposely tried to enjoy the various blessings the Lord put in a given day. For example, father–daughter dances at wedding receptions could be challenging. It was easy to be overcome by intense grief and tears, and sometimes I could not stop that. But when possible, I would get a grip on my emotions, purposely set the grief aside, and choose to focus on the joy of the bride and her father. In that situation, such a choice was not avoidance or denial; it was simply a practical way to be sensitive to others and to walk in faith by genuinely heeding the Lord's call to "rejoice with those who rejoice" (Romans 12:15).

At other times, when memories started the tears flowing, the best choice was to let them flow, to savor the memories even though they made the heartache more painful. It was tempting to flee from the pain by shoving the memory away and suppressing the emotions, but I think it was good to relish the tender remembrances and let the tears wash my aching heart, even if their saltiness stung its wounds.

Always it was good to remind myself that Jesus conquered death and gave us eternal life, and that those who have died in him are already living that wonderful life in heaven. We live a foretaste of it now, but they have woken up into its full glory. Al was seeing God face-to-face—something he had always longed to do—and worshiping him in all his breathtaking majesty. It was good to remember that.

I found that all three modes were necessary. If I had only lived in the busy present and never allowed myself to face the sorrow of Al's death, I would have become emotionally and spiritually crippled. Yet I did need to function in the present and walk by faith the path the Lord had put in front of me. If I had only dwelt in the grief, I would have been overwhelmed. Yet it was important to embrace and process that grief. And if I had only thought about heaven, I would have been so caught up with its glory that I would never have gotten anything done! However, I absolutely needed the hope and joy that came from knowing that Al was there and that I was heading there someday.

It might have been tempting to avoid any of the different modes, but if I wanted to be mentally, emotionally, and spiritually whole, all three were necessary.

# 81

## Embracing Joy and Sorrow

Several people in our family have had graduations since Al died: Eowyn and Alden from high school, Alasdair and I from seminary, Rebeckah from a graduate program, and Eowyn from college. They have each been bittersweet without Al here to celebrate them, and tears have been from both joy and sadness.

The only graduation I can tell you about from the graduate's perspective was my own (which also happened to be Alasdair's) from Westminster in May 2009. I suspect that aspects of it may be somewhat representative of the way each kid felt as he or she graduated.

As the time approached, I was intentionally not thinking much about the upcoming day. If I downplayed its significance in my own mind—if it was not a big deal—then maybe it wouldn't matter so much that Al wasn't there. I think I was subconsciously shielding my heart from something I knew was going to hurt a lot.

But as Alasdair and I drove together to the rehearsal the day before, he helped me let go of that self-protective stance and choose to say, "Yes, it's going to be a tough day and there will be lots of sadness and grief throughout it. But instead of distancing myself from fully feeling the joy of it so as to protect myself from fully feeling the grief, I will choose to face it head-on. I will fully embrace the happiness and sense of accomplishment of finishing the race I began, and fully embrace the sadness of Al not being there to see it." I had the sleeve of my academic gown well stocked with tissues.

Degrees are awarded by category from the highest to the lowest, so Alasdair received his degree before I did. It is tradition at WTS graduations for family members or friends in the audience to stand in honor of graduates as they are awarded their diplomas. So I stood for Alasdair, very aware that family members were also standing somewhere behind me and that Al was *not* there on stage standing for and beaming proudly at his son. (Nor was my mom there. She had hoped to attend graduation but died a month before.) But when I looked again, I saw Doug Green, Mike Kelly, and others of Al's colleagues on stage standing for Alasdair in Al's place. My tears started.

I had a little time to pull myself together before it was my turn. Just before my name was called, I took a deep breath and willed myself not to cry. But when I started across, a number of Al's colleagues on the faculty stood up, and I could barely breathe. That meant so much to me. They were my good friends, whom I had known for a long time and with whom I had walked through some hard things. In a way, I represented Al to them, and they were standing to honor the memory of a fallen comrade. And they also represented Al to me, and since their brother-in-arms was not able to be there to stand for his own family, they were standing in his place, in solidarity with both Al and me. It was precious, and excruciating, and wonderful all at the same time, and I definitely lost the battle against tears.

Toward the end of graduation we sang "For All the Saints." I've loved that hymn since I first became a Christian as a teenager, but in the context of all that had just happened, it meant more than ever. I thought of Al, who had lived a life of faith, following Jesus, the Captain he loved so much, and who was now at rest with him. I thought of him seeing the King of Glory face-to-face and of the "glorious day" when the saints will "rise in bright array" and join him in the King's presence. I could almost hear the "distant triumph song" even there in the auditorium.

It was bitterly, sweetly, joyfully, sorrowfully real, and I allowed my tender, hurting/healing heart to fully feel each of those emotions. I'm glad I refrained from shielding myself from the pain because I would have forfeited the joys. Instead, I entrusted my heart into the Lord's strong hands and let the deep, towering waves of both sets of emotions crash over it. In the end my heart was still safe in God's palms, cleansed and healthy from the saltwater.

# 82

# A Heart Laid Bare

In a class Eowyn took her senior year, they were given a flexible assignment to do an on-stage presentation with one other person about a life-changing event. It was a no-brainer what event had most changed Eowyn's life. I knew she was working on this project, but I didn't know the details. She invited me to observe on the day she presented, and I did.

Oh man.

One of Eowyn's good friends played Al, and besides being a really good sport to be involved at all, he did a good job playing the part. The fact that they had been friends since seventh grade made it more special, I thought.

Eowyn started out as a baby being rocked in Al's arms. Then she was a toddler, delightedly being chased around by him. Then he gave her a piggyback ride as a preschooler. Then he was teaching her how to ride a bike. (All this was effectively staged with minimal props and lots of imagination, and she kept adding, subtracting, or tweaking her costume to portray her aging self. There was music in the background, but no speaking.) Then Al and Eowyn were dancing.

Then, as her attention was diverted by some activity, he began to quietly and bravely show signs of pain and sickness and ended up lying on the floor. Eowyn wept over him as he died, but then he stood up again, climbed an eight- or ten-foot stepladder set farther back on the stage, and sat atop it, looking down on the ensuing scenes. Eowyn showed grief, anger, depression, listless apathy, quiet sadness.

Life events continued. She showed the audience a learner's per-
mit with great excitement, and Al rang a little bell from atop the ladder, but she couldn't hear it and her excitement quickly faded to sadness. Then she stood on a chair in cap and gown and cheered as she
graduated, and Al rang the little bell, but again her happiness faded
very quickly to grief. Then she appeared with flowers and a veil and
walked—alone—down the aisle for her wedding, with unheard bells
ringing from heaven, but she burst into tears and hurried off stage.

Then she came back on stage as a mature adult and interacted comfortably, smilingly, with imaginary people. But even as she mimed conversation with them, she began donning a white blouse. Once she had
it on, she happily gave them a casual wave goodbye, turned, went to
the ladder and climbed it. There she was welcomed by Al, who hugged
and held her and gave her the bell, which she rang with joy. Curtain.

I was a mess. I had bawled through the whole thing and I continued to bawl all the way back to the seminary, just in time to proctor a
midterm exam for a class in which I was the teaching assistant. Eowyn's
presentation was simple and profound. It laid open her heart, and all of
ours, for the world to see: the wonderful father Al was, the longing for
him, the sharp pain of his absence, the hope of heaven. It was simply,
vulnerably, and excruciatingly beautiful.

# 83

# A Fresh Wind

There was a music CD I listened to constantly in the car after Al died. Eventually I put it away and didn't listen to it until about three years later at Easter time. When the first notes of the first song started, they stirred the feelings, frame of mind, and memories from the weeks after Al's death. I remembered why that CD was so perfect for that time. It vibrates with praise to Jesus for what he's done. It marvels at the unbelievable grace that takes God's enemies and makes them his children. And it is awash with the glorious hope that we will one day stand in his presence and worship him face-to-face. I'm sure that one of the comforts of those songs at that time was knowing that this was exactly where Al was and what he was doing. He was where he had always looked forward to being. And I knew that someday we would join him and worship the Lord together again.

After Al died, my heart and mind were thinking of that glory all the time, and my ears were eagerly tuned to catch strains of heavenly voices singing along as I worshiped. The time and space between me and the heavenly throne room seemed like nothing at all—just the thinnest of veils and the briefest of moments that might be stepped through at any second.

As the months and years passed, the sense of the nearness of heaven gradually faded. But that night three years later, when I listened to the CD again, suddenly I was hearing it with the same sense of immediacy as I had before. I was keenly aware of the indescribable GLORY of Jesus and so bowled over by his unfathomable grace and mercy that I had to take off my rubber gloves, kneel right there on the kitchen floor, raise my hands in praise, and sing with everything in me. I don't know what the neighbors thought if they heard or saw me, but I didn't care. Thinking of what my Lord went through for me on the cross and what he won for me by his death and resurrection took my breath away. What a Savior! What a mind-blowing, history-altering thing that HE IS RISEN! The tomb is empty! All those wonderful Easter glories that we had just celebrated were true and real, and they made all the difference in everything.

Through the humdrum of daily life, as well as the high points and low points of the intervening three years, the reality of Jesus's victory over death had sustained us, given us hope, and brought joy in the midst of sadness. It was the rock on which we had stood and lived, and that rock was firm and unmoving. But as I said, that sense of the nearness of heaven had faded. So it was an unexpected treat that night to have my ho-hum mind-set blown right out the door by the wind of Easter and to experience once again the heart-stopping glory of a few moments worshiping at God's feet.

My focus was removed from grieving or even feeling close to Al as I worshiped. Instead, that night it seemed as if the curtain was drawn back and the brilliant light of heaven shone down like a spotlight into my kitchen. I was almost-as-good-as-there in his presence and overwhelmed by his grace. What filled my mind was, Jesus is so far above any words I could ever come up with to express his majesty that I can do nothing but sing my heart out and then marvel in silence.

# LOOKING BACK

# 84

# The Healing Process

Al has been gone for more than seven years now.

In the first months after he died, I remember picturing life as a stage and feeling as if his absence were an enormous mountain that filled the entire thing. Everything I did or thought happened in the small spaces around the edges. I expected that as time passed the mountain would gradually diminish and recede upstage until it became simply a two-dimensional painting on the backdrop, and that has indeed happened. I love Al as much as ever, and I miss him. But the grief does not dominate every waking moment anymore, though it's always there as part of the scenery. Being a widow is one piece of my identity. Most of the time I live in the present with joy and thankfulness, and both the sadness of missing Al and the anticipation of seeing him again in heaven remain in the background.

Before Al died, he reassured me, "The Lord will be with you, and he'll take care of you. All of you. I know our kids will bring you lots of joy, and I'm sure the Lord will bring new things into your life too— new interests and new ways to serve him." He wanted to be sure I knew that so that I wouldn't be anxious or fearful as I faced the future.

I knew that it pained him to think of leaving us behind without his love, care, and support, so I also reassured him, "We'll be okay. I know the Lord will watch out for us and provide for us. He will be here. I'm confident that he will take exquisite care of us." There is no doubt that he has certainly done so!

We have each processed our grief in our own time and our own ways. I'm so thankful that no one has rushed me. I think sometimes people try to hurry loved ones through their grief because it's hard to see them hurting. But my children and friends have given me space to take my time. It was comforting to me to have Al's things around, so I left some of his clothes in the closet and some of his things in the bathroom drawer for quite a while. In fact, it was probably five years before I cleared out the last of them, and when I did, I felt sad that whole day.

No one has tried to push me into dating, for which I am very thankful. Al's mom took me aside at one point to make sure I knew that it was fine with them if I started another relationship. Bless her! She is so incredibly thoughtful, and I can only imagine the strength it must require to say something like that. But I am not ready for that and I don't know if or when I will be. I am grateful that others have respected that.

The Lord did not demand that I do everything perfectly as I learned to be a single parent and run a household and a family by myself. Surprisingly, he enabled me not to demand it of myself either. He has also helped me learn the new skills I needed. And he has begun to give me opportunities to feel like a contributing member of society again.

Life in this world is bittersweet, with joy and sorrow mingled. But the Lord is in it all, redeeming the bitter and helping us to enjoy the sweet. The next four chapters talk a little bit about how the Lord has been with me in the bittersweetness of life.

# 85

## God and the Single Parent

I never expected to be a single parent.

Part of the beauty of parenting as a team is that you each bring differ-ent strengths to the job. Al was a *wonderful* father. If I had had to pick one of us to be left with the job of parenting our children alone and shepherd-ing them through grief and its consequences, for our kids' sakes I would certainly have picked him. Apparently the Lord thought differently.

During the spring of 2006, when Al was dying, I felt stressed about the prospect of parenting alone, and that was not without cause. In the months and years after Al's death, there were some trying periods for all of us. It was clear when Eowyn was sad or distressed—she talked about it. It was harder for Alden to do so. As I mentioned, he experienced a lot of unhappiness through junior high and high school, and we felt that.

When my dad was dying, a year after Al's death, I went to be with him and my mom and then stayed with her for a few days after his death. During the week I was gone, Alasdair/Lauren and Rebeckah took turns staying with Eowyn and Alden and keeping life running. By the time I got home, I discovered that tensions and frustrations were so high that it's amazing any of them were still speaking to each other. I vowed I would never go away from home again until Alden went to college.

Parenting, by its very nature, is full of judgment calls that you can always kick yourself for. When you're doing it alone, the weight of deci-sions feels even heavier. Thankfully, I wasn't truly alone. The Lord met me in the business of single parenting. The Bible sometimes describes the Lord as the husband of his people, and it always talks about him as our father. I knew he would be Father to my kids. I knew he loved them even more than I did and that he was committed to them even more than I was. I knew it broke his heart as much as it broke mine to see them hurting. I knew he would help me. And he did. He was with me and, one decision at a time (tentative on my part), *together*, we parented Eowyn and Alden through junior high and high school.

In addition I had the church family to help me. It seemed that when I was most at a loss for how to proceed, the Lord would arrange a "chance" meeting with another parent in the school parking lot, or at a soccer game, who would have just the right word of wisdom for that moment. God supplied other adults who loved, nurtured, guided, and prayed for my kids (and who prayed with and for me). That was a huge support. The kids each have adults in the church who are close to them.

Parenting grown children is a different task—one that can (and in my case probably did) get lost in the demands of parenting children who are still at home. Rebeckah was dealing with severe grief while simultaneously working a high-stress, thankless, under-staffed job. I wish I had been more active in loving and supporting her and Alasdair and Lauren. Since I wasn't, I am especially grateful for others who walked alongside them.

With God's help, we all survived. Eowyn and Alden made it to adulthood. When Alden went to college, he turned the reins of his life over to God, fell in love with Jesus, and has not looked back. He is one of the most wonderful, giving, humble, serving, loving, encouraging, thoughtful, Christlike young men I have ever known. When I hear and see the grace of God at work in his life, it blesses me beyond words.

I marvel at the Lord's grace to all of us. My children have become my peers, my friends, my brothers and sisters, and they are an indescribable blessing to me. All of us—now including two sons-in-law and a soon-to-be daughter-in-law as well—love each other very much. I not only love them, I also admire them and learn from them—I even seek them when I need wisdom, counsel, or prayer. I am so thankful. And I know Al would be proud too.

# 86

## Choosing Joy

From the time Al was diagnosed, it pained him to know that he would miss his children's weddings. Alasdair and Lauren had gotten married in 2004, and Al was thrilled and honored to co-officiate with Lauren's home pastor. When he talked about not being there for the weddings of the other three kids, it was hard for him to keep his sorrow in check. Just two days after Al's original diagnosis, Eowyn brought up the issue, and they cried together over the thought that he would not be there for her wedding. On the tumultuous day of Lisa Welch's wedding, Al and Rebeckah shared tears over the same grief. He would not be there, not walk them down the aisle, not officiate, not dance with them.

Both Rebeckah and Eowyn were married in 2013. We knew that their wedding days would be among the most bittersweet of all, and they were. Al's absence was keenly felt on each wedding day. But he was also "included" in the celebrations. Eowyn and Ben's choice of church was made possible because the pastor had known Al. I took pictures of Eowyn in her wedding dress by Al's grave. Rebeckah and Brian had little signs on the tables saying that in lieu of favors, they had given a donation to the Groves Center that was founded by and later named for Al. Alasdair and Alden danced with Eowyn in Al's place during the father-daughter dance (there was not a dry eye in the hall). Rebeckah and Brian chose the song "In My Life" for their first dance, which talks about never losing affection for people who have gone before. For me personally, the sorrow of Al being absent resulted in an unexpected blessing and privilege that few mothers get to experience: each of the girls asked me to walk them down the aisle and give them away. That is an honor that bowled me over and that I will cherish for the remainder of my life.

I did find that I was more emotional in general around the time of each wedding. The day following Eowyn and Ben's wedding, the Groves clan who had been able to attend the wedding gathered at a little farmhouse in Lancaster that Al's brother Warren rented. We had a lovely, relaxed afternoon together. Al would have been absolutely over the moon to have had nearly his whole extended family of four generations together in one place. I can't even put into words how much that would have meant to him. Toward the end of the afternoon, someone said, "Hey, we have to get a family picture." Since Al was always the one who insisted on that, it underscored the tragedy of his absence. It was indescribably sad that he was not there to enjoy the gathering. I had to slip off to the nearby field, lean against the far side of the cargo van I had rented, and just sob and sob out loud until I had cried my tears dry.

Although emotions were a bit closer to the surface than usual, I still smile when I think about how the Lord met us and blessed us in the girls' wedding days. Both days turned out to be happy, wonderful celebrations full of love from family and friends. For a long time there had been a dark cloud in the distance when we anticipated those days and wondered what they would be like; we had dreaded the intense grief we knew would be mixed with the great joy. The joy and the grief sat side by side in our hearts, and we accepted and fully felt both emotions. But the Lord met us, and joy won out.

# 87

# Grandchildren

During the first two years after Al's death we experienced a string of losses. Al died in February 2007. In March 2008, my dad died. In April 2009, my mom died. And one month later, another dear older relative with whom I was very close died. It was a rough couple of years. Yet, unsurprisingly, I feel Al's absence most in life's sweetest things.

We have celebrated multiple graduations. Various ones of us have had new jobs to be thankful for, and we have known that Al would be proud of each of us. I have been thankful to see us all healing and able to move forward with life, but there is always a pinch of grief that Al is not here to enjoy it.

And then, of course, there are the grandchildren. In 2009, our granddaughter Emily was born, and she completely owned all of our hearts from the get-go. Alasdair and Lauren moved to New Hampshire when Emily was one, but during her first fall, I got to take care of her on Tuesday mornings, and it was the uncontested highlight of every week. Sometime later my kids teased me that I was fifty-three and my best friend was a two-year-old. Now Emily has a little sister Adara—who is almost three as I finish editing this manuscript and who frequently has us all in stitches—and a little brother named for his uncle Alden, born this past spring 2014. Rebeckah and her husband Brian are expecting a son in February 2015. Perhaps there will be other grandchildren in the future. Each one is an indescribably precious gift and brings joy beyond bounds.

At the same time, it is a stabbing grief that Al isn't here to enjoy his grandchildren. His own grandparents were an important part of his life, and he had always looked forward to being a grandpa. When we learned that he had a year or two to live, knowing that he would never see his grandchildren was one thing he consistently had trouble talking about, because he got misty and choked up. I have a picture of him holding the newborn baby of some friends of ours about five weeks before he died, with an enormous smile of delight on his face. Even as I took the picture, I thought that that little tyke was standing in for any future grandchildren who might be born to us.

When Emily became old enough to look at photo albums, we realized that Al didn't have a name. He and I had never talked about whether he wanted to be "Grandpa," or "Poppy," or something else. It grieved me to think of Al being a nameless, unknown grandparent, like three of my own grandparents who were simply "Mommie's mother" or the like. But Alasdair decided Al would be "Grandpa Groves," and that is what the kids call him. I pray that they will each trust in Jesus and be united to him by faith. Then they will meet "Grandpa Groves" in heaven, and what a joyful meeting that will be!

# 88

## With God in the Dark

God has been with me in my various roles as a parent, as the mother of two brides, as a grandparent. But what if people ask, "What about *you* individually, just as yourself—a person, a woman, a single woman, apart from all other roles and relationships? What has this been like for *you* personally?"

I suppose the short answer is that I have not felt alone. Having gotten married at the age of twenty, I did not expect to be a single woman again at forty-nine. But the Lord has been so tenderly and tangibly with me, not only through wonderful people who have loved and supported me, but also in quiet, intimate ways—moments that no one else has shared, only the Lord and I. Let me briefly share five such times.

*One:* After my dad died in 2008, my mom, one of my sisters, and I accompanied his body to the crematorium an hour away. It was a sad time and we were all feeling pretty forlorn. We went to the hospital nearby where my dad had been a patient, so that my mom could thank the nurses and show us where he'd been. I remembered that Al's college roommate, whom we hadn't seen in years, might still work at that hospital, though probably not every day. It is a large complex, and I didn't know where his office was, nor if he would be there that day. I didn't think my mom was up to traipsing around looking for him, so I just quietly asked the Lord that if Tom happened to be there, he would have us run into him. Later, we happened to step into a random eatery, and Tom came in ten minutes later. Not only was it good to see him, it was also a tender, sharp reminder that the Lord was *there*—that he knew, that he cared, that he loved me.

*Two:* Eowyn started out riding the bus back and forth between Philly and Ohio for college, but it became clear that this was not safe, so we needed to buy her a used car. I know less than nothing about cars, so I am a prime candidate for getting hoodwinked in the used car business. But it occurred to me to pray about it. I was encouraged to pray boldly and specifically, so I did, and it was one of only two times in my life that I immediately knew the Lord had said "Yes." A long story followed, but I ended up finding a great, reliable car in good shape, at an affordable price, that has served her well ever since. From the moment I prayed, I felt as if the Lord was taking care of it and I was just along for the ride. The most remarkable thing of all was that I never once, for even one moment, felt like a vulnerable, solitary woman.

*Three:* I started teaching Hebrew at Westminster after I graduated in 2009. I *loved* my job from the first day. Especially in those early days following Al's death and when the empty nest arrived, it was an immeasurable blessing to me. At the end of 2011, with the economy struggling, we heard that there would be pay cuts and staff positions eliminated at Westminster. I fully expected my job to end, and I started thinking about what I might do next. It was a sobering process. In the end, my job remained, for which I was enormously thankful. But I am also thankful to have faced the possibility of being laid off. It forced me to think outside the box about what I might do next. It propelled me into exploring teaching English as a second language as a volunteer, and I love it! But the best thing was that, to my surprise, I never felt fearful or panicked. I knew the Lord would provide for us. I found that I *really believed* that whatever happened, the Lord would be in it, he would take care of us, and the next chapter might even be exciting. It was good to realize that even if I lost my job while I had two kids in college, we would be okay.

*Four:* I sort of dreaded the arrival of the empty nest. That was already true long before Al's cancer. I *loved* being a mother, and I knew that there would be a large dose of sadness when all the children were gone from home, even though it would be nice for Al and me to have time to enjoy each other without parenting responsibilities. In 2006 we had a foretaste of the empty nest years while the kids were away for a few days, and that made me realize that when the day came in 2011, it was going to hit with double sadness—I would be minus my children and also minus the opportunity to spend more time with my husband.

But in the Lord's providence, in June 2011 I broke and mangled my ankle so badly that by late August, when Alden went off to college, I was still getting around with a walker. I was not able to fully put weight on the ankle and was using much of my mental and physical energy just to accomplish the daily tasks of life. I was sleeping on a cot off the kitchen, with my clothes hung all over the place and everything discombobulated. Thus Alden's leaving felt more like another large wrinkle in the general abnormality of things rather than the sole alteration. I really think that softened the transition for me. Destroying an ankle is not the way one expects to see the Lord's tenderness, but it really was thoughtful of him. Of course I only recognized that thoughtfulness in retrospect, but when I did, I had a private chat with the Lord and thanked him. I could almost imagine him smiling at the fact that I finally had eyes to discern the gift he had given me months before. It was another of those shared moments.

*Five:* There have been things in the lives of people I love that left me feeling very heavy-hearted. It was at those moments that I missed Al most keenly. How I would have loved to talk to him about them, to get his wisdom, to cry in his arms. But he was not there, and I couldn't talk to another living soul about it. So I sat alone and held those people in my heart and prayed. And then I got up and kept going with the heaviness.

But when I went to the Lord as I would have gone to Al, the Lord was *there*. He walked with me on the days when my heart was heavy, and he encouraged me that he is a God who redeems broken people and broken situations. One night I felt concerned and discouraged about a situation, so I turned off all the lights and sat in a rocking chair in the dark living room and prayed. As I did, I had such a sense of the Lord's mighty, glorious majesty. He was there in power and awe, the Creator of the universe, mighty to rule and mighty to save. *He* was the God who was my Father and who loved and cared for me and for the people I loved. Remembering that put everything into perspective. In situations where there was nothing I could do to help, I could pray, and in fact, praying was probably the most helpful thing. I was not alone at all. In the times I had no one I could talk to except the Lord, I realized more clearly than ever how close and real he was, and that he listened and cared. He was (and is!) *always* there to talk with me.

Looking back I realize that those moments of the Lord reminding me of his tender, intimate love and nearness are actually the highlights of these years, and some of my most precious memories.

# 89

# Grief Undone

That brings us to the present time. The story will continue, but this is as much as I know now.

I am amazed at how the Lord really has "undone" our grief. That didn't happen in an instant; it was an ongoing, unfolding process. And it doesn't mean that there has been no pain. We have felt the deep heartbreak of losing Al. We've ached, and cried, and missed him terribly. But we have also known the deeper, truer underlying reality that Al is with our Lord, experiencing life and glory such as we can only imagine, and that has made all the difference.

The other thing that has made all the difference is God being with us. That's what "Immanuel" means. God's care for us has indeed been exquisite, just as (in faith) I assured Al it would be. I've often heard people say that through suffering they got to know God much better, and that has certainly been true for me in losing Al. This is not the road I would have chosen. But I have seen the Lord's phenomenal, overwhelming, unfailing, tender, protective, faithful love as I never had before, and I know him and have grown close to him in ways I'm sure I wouldn't have otherwise. That is something I wouldn't trade away. Honestly, this has been one of the most vibrant and glory-filled periods of my life.

Jesus "undid" grief definitively by his own once-for-all death and resurrection, but the way he works that out in each grieving person's situation is different. In many ways our circumstances were easier than those of others, yet I know that the Lord will meet each person in his or her unique suffering.

As I've said, we were spared the emotional roller coaster that so many cancer patients have to ride, hoping that a treatment will work and then struggling with disappointment or despair if it doesn't. But I have dear young friends who have been on that roller coaster for the past five years, and I have seen the Lord faithfully sustain them in the midst of it.

We knew Al was going to die, and we had plenty of time to make arrangements in advance and to say all the things we wanted to say to him before he died. But sometimes death comes suddenly, without warning, and there is no chance to say that last "goodbye" or "thank you" or "I love you." Plus, the family left behind then has to deal with the overwhelming details of funeral and burial arrangements in the midst of shock and grief. Yet somehow the Lord gives the strength to get through that too, as he did recently for my good friend Susan.

We were blessed to walk together as a family in love and closeness and were spared the heartrending, complicated grief of losing a child, or facing a suicide, or losing someone in a challenging relationship. Yet I have seen the real grace and strength of God sustain friends who faced all three of those factors.

We had phenomenal support from a host of people near and far who loved and helped and encouraged us. How much harder it is to be alone and isolated as you die or as you watch a loved one die. Yet in those times, knowing that the Lord, the God and Creator of the Universe, sits quietly with you and wraps his strong arms around you must be precious comfort. The night I spent sitting in my rocking chair, alone in the dark with just the Lord to talk to, was one of the most special nights of my life.

Finally, knowing God as our Father—a loving, merciful, generous, faithful, kind Father—made a difference every single day for Al and for us. And knowing that Jesus had defeated death and opened the way to heaven for his people took the sting out of death and undid our grief. I ache for people who face death—their own or a loved one's—without the companionship of God or the hope of heaven. Thankfully, God's family is not exclusive; the Father is *delighted* to welcome people into it. In fact, Jesus died precisely to make that possible. If you are facing grief without God, please know that he will be glad to welcome you into his family, even now. That's why Jesus died: to pay for our sins so we could come to the Father. Just ask! May you find a warm welcome into the comforting arms of the Father and of his people.

May the Lord walk with you on your journey. If you are facing death—your own or a loved one's—or grief of another kind, I pray that you too will experience the Father's presence and tender love, that all the blessings that flow out of Jesus's death and resurrection will sustain you and heal your heart, and that you too will find your grief coming undone.